Local SEO
The Blueprint

For Home Service Business Owners

Matt Miciula, MBA

Second Edition
ISBN (Paperback): 978-1-7381272-0-7
ISBN (e-book): 978-1-7381272-1-4

Digital Shift
https://www.getdigitalshift.com

DISCLAIMER
The information contained within this book is intended to provide readers with a general overview of Search Engine Optimization (SEO) principles and practices. While we have made every effort to ensure the accuracy and relevance of the information presented, it is crucial to understand that the field of SEO is dynamic and constantly evolving. This book does not serve as a substitute for professional SEO advice, and it is highly recommended to consult with qualified SEO professionals or experts for specific, tailored guidance.

DEDICATION

To all the home service owners who strive to grow their business and create a positive impact in their community

CONTENTS

ACKNOWLEDGMENTS

The team at Digital Shift would like to take this opportunity to thank all of our loyal customers and partners, particularly those who have been with us since Day One in 2007. As your marketing and SEO experts for the last 17 years, we are honored to be a crucial part of your business journey and will continue to make every effort to serve you in the best ways possible for the years ahead.

INTRODUCTION

Marketing is the essence of every business, from providing detailed and transparent information to selling and meeting a customer's needs and expectations. The purpose of every product and service is to offer optimal solutions to problems that your customers cannot solve on their own. Merely having the solutions on hand won't guarantee you any success or visibility in your area unless you invest in a strategic digital marketing solution.

Home service providers offer a wide range of maintenance, repair, improvement, and remodeling services. This means that skills, workmanship, and customer service play a huge role in delivering positive results for any requested service. As the business owner, you know which attributes to target for excellence and hiring the right marketing team will help elevate your main services, highlight your team's strengths, and outrank your competitors in Google's search engine.

But what kind of digital marketing is SEO? How do you make your business known and visible to the local public?

At Digital Shift, we want to earn the right to do business with you and hope this book will inspire you and open up a path of great business opportunities. In the chapters ahead, you will learn about the key ingredients of building an effective marketing strategy involving SEO optimization, content creation, Google profile management, social media, and more! But first, here's a bit about what makes us one of North America's leading authorities on SEO.

Our Story:

Digital Shift is a Canadian online marketing agency. Since 2007, we have been helping businesses discover online opportunities that complement their vision, making long-term success a reality. Our company has continued to grow through client referrals and by assisting new and growing businesses. Our vision is to be the go-to search engine optimization experts for home service businesses. The online solutions we provide include all the integral components needed to help local businesses be found and become popular online. Over the years, Digital Shift has helped many small, medium-sized, and franchise businesses become aware of and fulfill the many online opportunities necessary for success.

Our marketing and SEO experts are determined to help your business grow. We are here to assist you with all your digital marketing, business strategy, advertising management, and branding needs. From managing Google profiles to SEO keyword optimization, geo-targeting for local customers, and social media posting to maximize brand exposure, we offer fast and secure digital marketing solutions for your business.

For more information, please visit

https://www.digitalshift.pro or call 888-380-2260.

We look forward to helping you make the shift and grow your business!

Sincerely,

Matt Miciula, MBA
CEO & Co-founder

August 2024

CHAPTER 1: WHY IS SEO IMPORTANT FOR HOME SERVICE BUSINESSES?

In this chapter, we will look at how SEO:

- Improves visibility of your business online
- Attracts targeted traffic to your website
- Builds authority and trust
- Is a cost-effective marketing strategy

Many home service businesses stumble upon "Search Engine Optimization" (SEO) while looking for new strategies to scale their business and drive new customers. In this kind of industry, it is crucial that you know your local community and its needs. The ultimate goal is to draw attention to your services and the values you bring.

You might wonder how optimizing your online presence for search engines can improve your business. SEO provides many benefits for home service businesses with a clear idea of who their target audience is—namely, local residents. Understanding why SEO is important for businesses is the key to getting all those benefits and utilizing a proven SEO strategy.

Obtaining and implementing all the necessary information, tools, and tactics involved in SEO can feel like an overwhelming learning curve. This is where trained SEO experts take over and provide you with the best SEO tactics to improve your organic traffic, which refers to authentic website traffic from potential customers through unpaid search engine results. By adding SEO to your overall marketing strategy, you will get everything you need to boost your marketing efforts.

In this chapter, you will learn why SEO is important for home service businesses and how a well-organized SEO campaign can be an absolute goldmine for your business.

Are you ready to help your local business improve its search engine rankings? Let's dive in.

Top Reasons Why SEO Is Important for Your Business

SEO Improves Your Visibility

1. Improves your company's visibility on search

engines like Google
2. Attracts more website traffic, generating more leads and sales
3. Generates local awareness by being part of Google's top local map pack

Homeowners search for home services online these days, which means that home service businesses like yours must be visible to your potential clients. When people search for a service you offer, you want to be at the top of the page in the search results. Or better, you want to be featured as the "local pack" on the Search Engine Result Page (SERP), which means you're one of the top three listed in response to the most relevant search queries. This way, you're more likely to connect with potential customers in desperate need of the services you provide.

However, there's more to improving visibility than just being the first business people see. On Google's search result pages, one of the first things searchers see is a list of paid ads. These are displayed at the top of the page, showing the names of the companies that paid for Google Ads to rank at the top. While paid ads such as LSA and PPC ads increase visibility and can provide a quick boost to local businesses, they're not always where most clicks come from, nor are they a standalone long-term solution for consistent traffic and leads, especially with every cost increase year over year.

Paid Ads are at the very top of Google's search results page and are classified into two categories: Local Services Ads (LSA) and Pay-Per-Click Ads (PPC).

Local Services Ads: LSA offers quick lead generation for specific service industries with advantages such as rapid results and pay-per-lead pricing. Their verification process provides a level of trust and legitimacy. However, they come with limited control as well as limited customization and Google-managed aspects compared to PPC.

Pay-Per-Click Ads: A PPC campaign has its place in online marketing as a way to pay top dollar for immediate leads. But it's important to note that the majority of the traffic potential and leads come from ranking in the top organic positions. Thus, PPC delivers only a short-term boost, whereas SEO provides more long-term results. However, both are useful for a well-rounded strategy.

The image below shows a heat map from a case study completed by BrightLocal evaluating what users click on from the search engine results page. This case study evaluates over 5,000 users to determine how users choose local businesses in Google searches.

It's clear that the organic search results and local pack results are where most clicks come from—over 70%, in fact. These organic search results are where you want to be most visible.

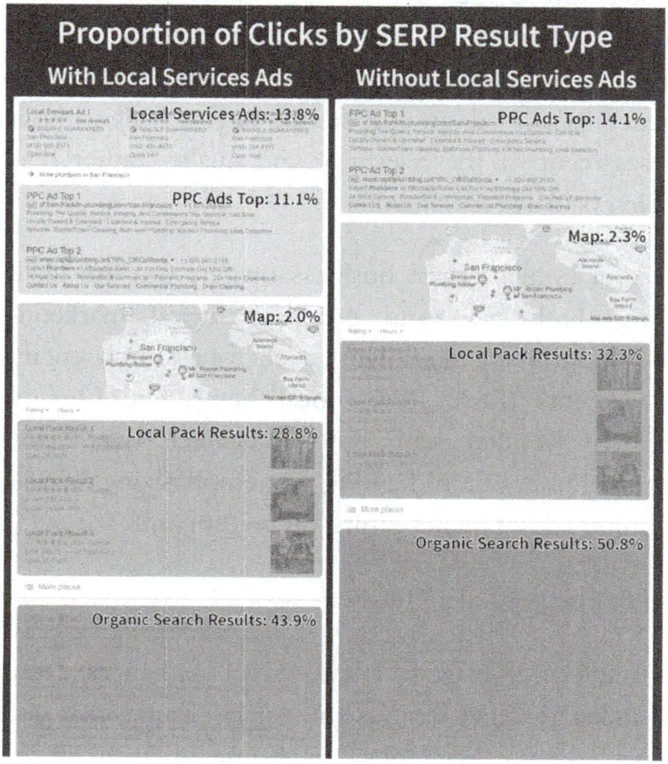

Let's break down exactly what local pack and organic search results mean for your business.

Local Pack Results: The local pack, also referred to as "map pack" or "local 3-pack," is a section that displays a set of three local businesses or services related to the user's search query in a map format, along with key details like business names, addresses, phone numbers, and ratings.

Organic Search Results: These are the rank results directly below the maps. Many users see these as earned positions and find them credible. These listings are considered "organic" because they are generated based on the search engine's algorithmic assessment of the relevance and quality rather than being paid advertisements.

As a home service business owner, you are likely using both paid and non-paid digital marketing methods. Being dominant in all four search engine placements (LSA, PPC, Local Maps, and Organic Search Results) can put a blanket over your competition, but in the long run, emphasizing organic results yields a higher return on investment.

Let's explore SEO further:

Actively managed Local SEO enhances your visibility through various means. It ensures that you have an up-to-date business listing in each of the major business directories that are relevant to your industry. And it ensures your Google Business Profile (formerly Google My Business) is accurate and kept relevant with posts, images, and review responses.

Benefits Of Targeted Traffic

Let's now take a look at targeted traffic and cost-effective marketing, two ways SEO works to benefit your business.

- Rank for specific keywords relevant to your business
- Receive clicks from ideal customers
- Create high-quality content relevant to your services
- Attract targeted traffic to your website (visitors who are already interested in your products or services)
- Increase the chances of converting visitors into paying customers

In essence, targeted traffic means high-quality leads. This can be achieved through detailed keyword research, quality content creation, and improved user experience (UX) for desktop and mobile traffic. Other ways to get targeted or branded traffic include obtaining search signals, such as backlinks from trusted sources and building local citations—all of which are integral to good SEO practices.

Targeted traffic provides a number of opportunities for conversions and sales and boosts the chances of generating revenues and profits. Every home service provider aims to achieve higher conversion rates and generate repeated sales.

Cost-Effective Marketing

- Create a marketing strategy targeting people who are already looking for your services

- Save money on advertising and marketing costs
- Drive organic traffic and generate leads affordably
- Incorporate keywords into your marketing and advertising

All local businesses know the importance of marketing, whether it's the business owner, a small marketing team, a marketing department that's a part of a franchise, or a marketing partner. All businesses need to have someone in charge of developing brand awareness and increasing the company's online visibility. Back in the day, the time-consuming approach included tons of costly advertising. But you can create cost-effective marketing strategies with SEO tactics. Integrate SEO into your email marketing, social media, and even your Google Business Profile.

SEO can also complement your paid advertising strategy. For instance, it's possible to retarget ads with optimized keywords based on your organic visitors. This way, you re-engage and retarget your customers from a fresh perspective. You can also use this strategy to attract previous visitors who never converted to a lead on your website.

SEO Builds Authority and Trust

- Build credibility for your business. Highly-ranking businesses are more trustworthy and credible to searchers
- Consistent top rankings create a sense of reliability
- Top-ranked pages attract more clicks, reinforcing trust

Connecting with potential new customers by reaching the top spot on Google is great, but it's not the only reason why SEO is important. It's also not the only thing you need to convert potential customers into satisfied customers. With SEO, your potential customers will be more likely to choose your services if they believe your business is trustworthy. A high level of trust enhances your website's reputation and authority, which is also backed by quality content.

Sitting in the top spot on Google's search results is a powerful way to build trust and authority about your particular industry. Ensure that you closely follow Google's quality guidelines for "Experience, Expertise, Authority, and Trust" (EEAT or "Double EAT") in order to retain that spot. You can learn more about this in Chapter 7.

But that's not the only way that SEO boosts your authority and trustworthiness.

One of the key SEO strategies for improving organic traffic to a website is to create customer-focused and value-added content that is engaging and relevant. Online searchers are attracted to blog posts because they want to learn something new and discover new trends in an industry. This is what your potential customers will want to seek out.

An effective SEO strategy isn't just about creating any content with relevant keywords and topics, although that's certainly an integral part of it. Creating quality content demonstrates your overall expertise, which helps you build authority and trust. This promotes positive search experiences that resonate with both Google and your potential customers.

SEO Keeps You Competitive

- Gives you a competitive edge by standing out from competitors
- Attracts new customers and retains existing ones
- Attracts more traffic with a well-optimized website
- Generates more leads and sales than your competitors
- Helps measure competitor's performance and compare it to yours

If you're not able to reach those top spots on Google's search results, you'll miss out on a large chunk of online search traffic that could be directed your way. Ensuring you use an SEO campaign to improve your organic visibility will help you stay competitive with other businesses in your area. They are likely using their own strategies to appeal to online search engine algorithms and searchers.

There are numerous best practices and techniques when it comes to organic search results. Businesses that use a digital marketing strategy to tailor their user experience and online presence to the needs of people searching for their services have better chances of connecting with high-quality leads. They will also have more success converting those online searchers into paying customers.

The "Hows" of SEO

How SEO Supports Brand Development

- Gives your business an identity
- Enhances the company's image, services, and products
- Increases domain authority score
- Drives a positive user experience
- Builds long-term brand equity

Making a business known to the public is difficult enough for most home service companies, much less making it a household name. One of the key benefits of effective SEO is that it supports ongoing brand development by promoting and helping to create the identity of your business.

Consistently appearing high up in organic rankings is the best foundation for promoting your brand and ensuring that people can find you online. This provides a big branding boost for home service companies in industries where people are often searching for services online—which involves nearly every industry today. But as mentioned previously, it also helps promote your brand's authority and trustworthiness.

Your engaging blog posts and other high-quality content will build brand awareness. In other words, they help establish and support the voice and identity of your business and brand—both in the format and style of your content.

High-quality and relevant content also gives you the opportunity to engage with your prospective customers before they need your services. You'll also increase your website's domain authority, which is a search engine factor score developed by Moz that search engines use to measure your website's relevance and success in the search results.

Digital marketing efforts that also include managing your Google Business Profile and actively asking for and responding to reviews—both positive and negative—will help you engage with your current customers and further establish your brand's identity, voice, and values.

How SEO Promotes Long-Term Growth

- Generates long-term revenue and other improvements
- Compounds and builds up brand equity over time
- Provides long-term benefits consistently (unlike paid advertising, which stops working once you stop paying for it)

When optimizing your website and creating high-quality, relevant content consistently, you can maintain your search engine rankings over time and continue to attract new visitors to your site.

It's important to ensure that your marketing strategies will not only improve your business today but also continue to provide benefits well into the future. Strategies like paid ads are great for providing a short-term boost or retargeting prior visitors. However, they will work even better when you can transition that boost into long-term growth with a robust digital marketing strategy that includes SEO practices.

In terms of marketing strategies that support long-term growth, SEO is one of the best. That's because search engine optimization is an ongoing process. The best practices for improving your visibility to online traffic are constantly evolving, and this requires you to stay on top of Google's updates and ever-changing algorithms. Ongoing, effective SEO efforts will continually provide benefits that help you grow your client base, build your brand, and improve your online visibility.

How to Combine SEO With Content Marketing

- Mix the natural with the technical
- Leverage existing assets like content, images, and videos
- Benefit from long-term ROI

One of the best parts about SEO is that you can easily integrate it with your existing marketing strategies. It helps provide better results for both your existing marketing mix and your new search engine optimization efforts. There's no need to sacrifice one for the other. In fact, the effects of exceptional SEO are even better when improvements created by SEO—like a better user experience on your website—are given visibility and support from other marketing efforts. For instance, content marketing that involves blogs, videos, or eBooks is an inbound strategy that drives traffic organically. Here, the rule is to make your content readable, well-structured, and well-formatted so Google recognizes the quality. And by weaving in SEO, you double your chances of being found by potential customers.

So besides naturally creating engaging, relevant content with SEO, you are including high-ranking keywords, search engine signals, and internal links. The right SEO content marketing strategy keeps you competitive and brings long-term growth with an attractive return on investment. Plus, you'll always benefit from increased traffic and brand awareness.

Conclusion

SEO is a valuable tool for home service businesses to succeed in their local area. As the competitive digital world continues to evolve, SEO becomes increasingly important if you want to thrive and stay on top of the competition.

In this chapter, you learned why SEO is important, and here is a little summary to take away. The reasons why SEO is important for your business include the following:

- Improve your local visibility on primary search engines, such as Google, Bing, or Yahoo.
- Achieve targeted traffic and high-quality leads when using detailed keyword and topic research.

- Spend less money on online ads when choosing SEO as your cost-effective marketing strategy.
- Know the Google quality rater guidelines and EEAT "Experience, Expertise, Authority, and Trust" to remain credible and trustworthy to your target audience

Stay competitive, compare your competitors' performance to your own, and fix any weak spots.

CHAPTER 2: HOW DO YOU OPTIMIZE YOUR GOOGLE BUSINESS PROFILE FOR SUCCESS?

This chapter focuses on:

- Google Maps ranking factors
- Optimizing your Google Business Profile (formerly Google My Business or GMB)
- Importance of selecting correct primary and secondary categories
- Impact of showing vs. hiding your address
- Google Business Profile features

Are you making the most of your Google Business Profile (GBP)? Most businesses can create their own Google Business Profile. However, it takes some consistent effort to become visible. If you want to be seen by prospective customers and appear prominently in organic search results, you'll need to properly optimize your GBP.

Optimizing your Google Business Profile isn't just essential for making sure you appear higher in Google search rankings and on Google Maps. It's also to make sure your business is more easily found by potential customers in your area. Great optimization can even help convert potential customers into happy customers by promoting your business's brand and values.

Thankfully, setting up and optimizing your GBP doesn't have to be complicated.

An expert SEO company like Digital Shift can help optimize and manage your Google Business Profile. But there's also a lot of optimization you can get done on your own before handing the reins over to an SEO company. If you're ready to get started, but are wondering exactly how to optimize your GBP, our SEO experts are here to assist.

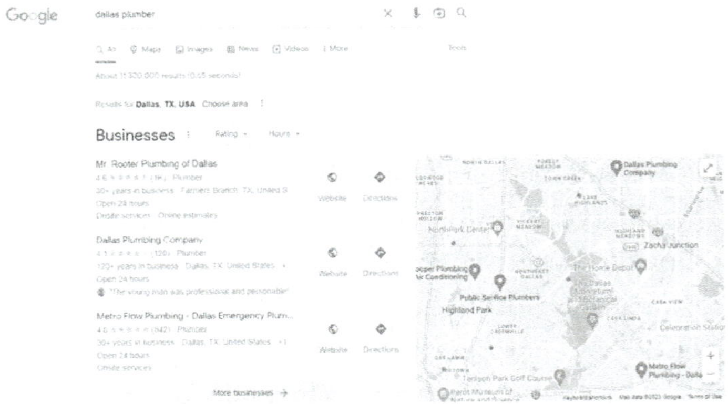

Why Should You Optimize Your Google Business Profile?

Although there are many factors to ranking in maps, Google uses three main factors when it compares online searches with existing profiles to determine rankings: relevance, distance, and prominence.

It's important to ensure your business and profile are correctly optimized for each of these three factors. Otherwise, customers may not be able to see or contact your business.

Relevance: Relevance refers to how your Google Business Profile matches with people searching for the services you offer in the area. Your services become relevant when people regularly search for your type of business. So optimizing your profile accordingly for the right services and the relevant categories will improve your ranking and visibility.

Distance: Distance or proximity is simply how far your business location or address is from the location of the person doing a search. Potential customers might be searching for "(Your service) + near me," So depending on how far you're willing to travel or how profitable the area is, you could be increasing your GBP proximity with Google Maps SEO. As a general rule of thumb, businesses located closer to the searcher's location are more likely to rank higher—

but this is not the only factor that contributes to a higher search rank.

PRO TIP: being physically closer to your target households, especially if your address is visible on your Google Profile, will help maximize your changes or ranking on Google Maps within that area.

Prominence: Prominence is based on signals created by parts of your profile, like credible online mentions on the web, backlinks, number of quality reviews, and your review score. These factors highlight how popular your business is in your local community and the overall engagement and visibility of the business across the web. People type in your brand name because they specifically seek your service in their area. Prominence is a significant category that can benefit greatly from proper search engine optimization.

Managing Your Google Profile

The Google profile is managed directly from Google search when you are logged into the Google account that has access. Profile features and editing options are only visible to managers and owners of the account.

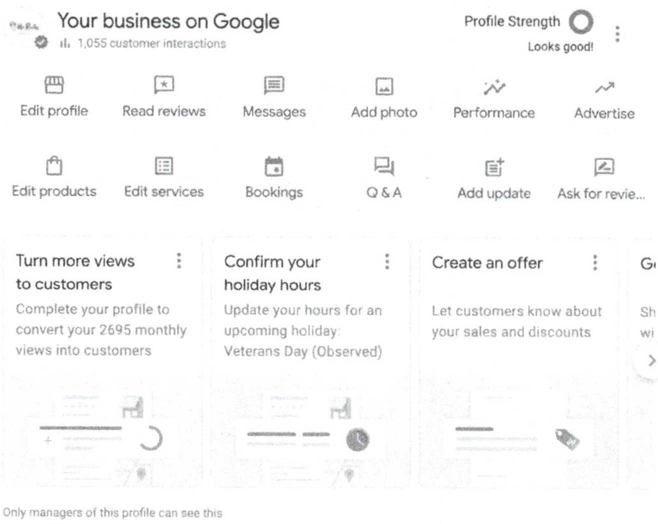

Primary owners of the account have full control over who can access the profile and add and remove other owners and managers. Owners can add or remove users, except for the Primary owner. Managers of the profile have access but cannot add or remove users. If you have multiple locations, you can see all the profiles from the Google Business Profile Manager by typing into your web browser: https://business.google.com/

Enter Your Business Information

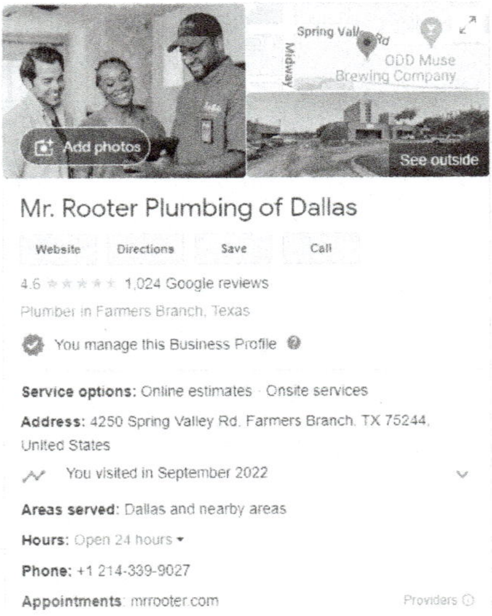

You can access your business information section by clicking the first button on your business dashboard once you've navigated to your Google Business Profile. The first step towards optimizing your profile's information properly is to ensure it has all the important information any prospective customer needs to know. From your business name and physical address to your phone number and operating hours, you should make sure the details entered are accurate and up-to-date.

Some sections on the business information page allow you to add more information, such as your business's unique offerings, culture, mission, and values. You may also include that information in your business description, so you don't have to fill out each and every section.

With that said, there are a few key sections you want to fill out properly. Discover these must-haves for your GBP:

Google Business Profile Address

The decision to show or hide your address is now more significant for rankings and visibility on Google Maps. Google trusts businesses with physical addresses more. When your address is visible, Google uses it to determine your proximity to prospective searchers. If it's hidden, Google considers you a Service Area Business, and you will be less likely to appear prominently in local map searches. Google may revert to the original verification address, which could misrepresent your service area. A physical address can also build trust and credibility for your brand from prospective customers.

PRO TIP: Showing your address on your Google profile enhances visibility, but make sure you follow Google guidelines so potential customers can find you more easily.

Set Your Categories

Setting your primary category and adding relevant secondary categories is one of the most important parts of optimizing your Google Business Profile. Not only will it impact relevance and affect how you appear in local search results, but it will also affect some additional features that may be available to you in Google's profile manager. For example, home service businesses can display a list of their services in their Google Business Profile. This will appear underneath your business information as "Services."

The Primary Business Category

When choosing a primary category, you will have to select from the list of available categories generated by Google—you cannot create your own. The category should be as specific as possible while still accurately representing your business. For example, if you exclusively provide handyman services, it is better to select "handyman" than something like "contractor" as your primary category. If you provide a wide range of services, you have the ability to add nine additional sub, or secondary categories, to your profile.

Secondary Business Categories

Use your secondary business categories to provide more specific indications of the types of services you provide. If you're a handyman who provides siding services, you might add "siding contractor" to your secondary categories. Ensure that the secondary categories you select are still relevant to your primary category to help Google and users better understand what you do.

PRO TIP: Changing your categories and Google profile services based on seasonality keeps your business profile up-to-date and well-optimized.

Complete Your Business Description

The business description on your Google Business Profile is more than just a basic company description. It's your opportunity to provide an overview of the services or products you offer, plus your company's values. With a restriction of 750 characters, it's best to keep your description accurate and concise with optimized keywords. Instead of selling your service in the description, you want to focus on solving a problem and why you are the perfect candidate for it.

Your business description plays a major role in relevance when Google evaluates your profile. It does so to see how you match with online searches, so it's important to add key information that describes your services here. Otherwise, your profile might not seem as relevant as those of businesses that have completed their description.

PRO TIP: Write an engaging description that clearly outlines who you are, what you do, the areas you serve, how you can help, and why homeowners should choose you.

Contact information: Add a primary phone number and, if applicable, a secondary phone number. If you have an alternate phone number or an old number, this is a good place to add it, so Google can better understand your business information online.

Website: Add a website URL that directs the searcher straight to your localized page. If you are a multi-location business or franchise, use a geo link relevant to your business's location. You can also add a UTM (Urchin Tracking Module) in your URL to record the traffic coming via your GBP in Google Analytics. UTMs are small snippets of code that you add to the end of your URL to track your marketing efforts' performance.

For example, adding a tracking code after the link is common for home services:

- **Website URL**:
yourwebsite.com/?utm_source=gmb&utm_medium=organic&utm_campaign=local

- **Appointment URL**:
yourwebsite.com/booking/?utm_source=gmbappt&utm_medium=organic&utm_campaign=local

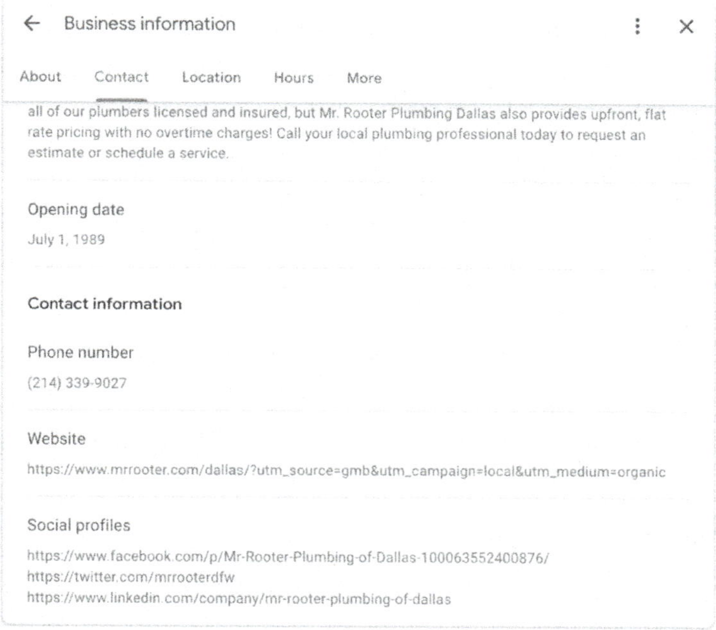

Social Profiles: Google Business Profile now lets you associate your social media profile with your listing. You can add Facebook, Instagram, LinkedIn, Pinterest, TikTok, X (formerly known as Twitter), and YouTube. Google may add social media links to eligible Business Profiles automatically, but you can log in and edit this information.

Areas Served: Include the areas you serve and list them in your profile. Doing so will also display the service area map on your profile if your business is a service area business (the address is not publicly displayed on your Google profile). You can list up to

20 areas, including counties, cities, and specific zip codes. If you are a large service area business, it's good practice to start with the larger territories first, like counties and cities, before drilling down and adding neighborhoods and zips. This is because it can be more helpful for potential customers to know the entire area you serve on your Google profile.

PRO TIP: Ensure you are maximizing the "Areas Served," especially if you have your address hidden on your profile, as Google may revert to the original verification address, which could misrepresent your service area.

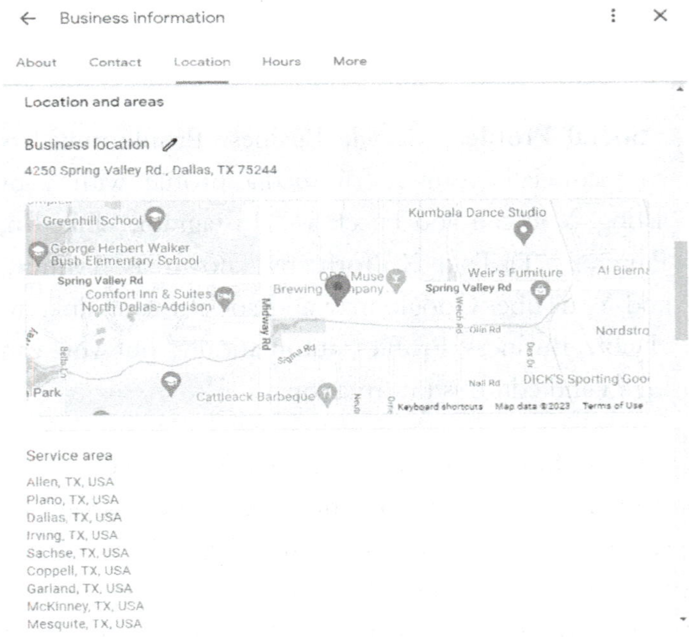

Business Hours: Indicating accurate hours of operation will prevent customers from contacting you or showing up at your office when you're closed. This includes accurate information about holiday hours and other special hours. Are you available 24/7 for emergencies? If yes, ensure that office phone calls are redirected to an emergency contact. Otherwise, it could result in a negative customer experience. Incorrect hours can make a prospective customer and Google lose trust in your business. The results in Google Maps can vary depending on the time of day and your business availability.

In some cases, it may make sense to use the "more hours" option on your profile. For example, if you have a store that sells parts and is open from 9-5 but provides after-hour support 24/7. In this case, you could keep your regular business hours and add additional business hours, such as "online service hours," as available 24 hours.

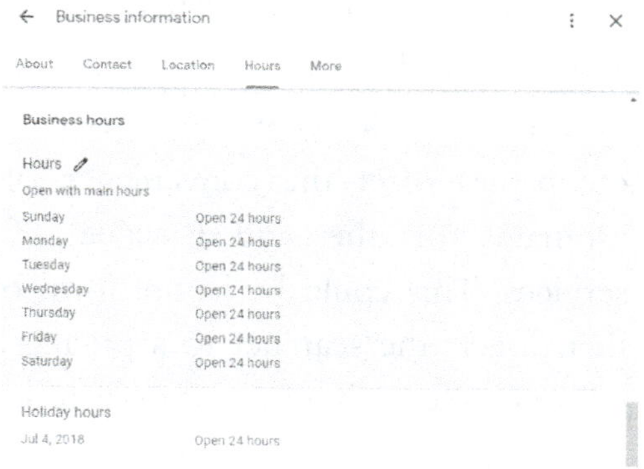

PRO TIP: Business hours can influence your visibility in local search results. Not being open when your competitors are can push down your Maps results for prospective searchers outside of your regular business hours.

Include Additional Business Information

The more information you can add to your Google Business Profile, the better optimized it will be, as long as the information you add is relevant, factual, and accurate. Be sure to fill out any remaining empty sections if relevant information is still missing.

Some additional business information you may want to list includes:

- **Opening date**: Indicating when you started your business shows the years of experience you bring.
- **Short name**: If your business has a shortened version of its name, add it here, so it registers as a potential keyword.
- **Online estimates/onsite services**: Some companies offer the convenience of online estimates or the added value of onsite services. This could be in the form of a link that directs the searcher to a pricing list or a job request estimate form for onsite services.

- **More information**: In this section, you're free to include info on accessibility, amenities, crowd, payment details, and other offerings your customers may find useful.

Ultimately, the more information you add to the business information section of your GBP, the better you'll match up with relevant searches for your products or services.

Respond To Your (Old) Reviews

Online reviews have a strong connection to your prominence and overall popularity on Google. That includes not just your review score on Google, but also how promptly you respond to reviews and the rate at which you accumulate reviews (known as review velocity).

If you have older customer reviews that you have not responded to, they can have a negative effect on your prominence and, therefore, your ranking. Even a positive review without a response can have this effect, so it's important to read through your reviews and respond to each of them.

Responding to negative reviews is especially important for your branding and reputation. Put yourself in your customer's position and acknowledge their disappointment. Take responsibility and apologize for their less-than-ideal customer service experience (if appropriate), but remain professional and courteous and offer an opportunity to connect offline to discuss further. You can also work on a potential solution to make up for their negative experience.

Add Images To Your Google Business Profile

At the very least, you should have a few relevant business photos on your profile. Be sure to add a logo as well as a cover photo—both should be consistent with your brand colors based on your branding. These images can help you stand out more and increase your brand awareness and trustworthiness.

You can also upload photos, videos, and images related to your business and the services you provide or products you sell. For example, a carpenter might add images of their completed work, while a plumbing company might add images of their plumbers during a pipe repair. You may also want to create and upload before and after photos, infographics, promotional images, and other images that accurately reflect your business.

It's best to restrict yourself to using original, high-quality photos and optimized and localized images. They don't have to be taken by a professional photographer, and most phones these days will do the trick.

Just ensure that images are clear and not blurry or distorted. The more interesting and engaging the images, the more likely you are to increase your prominence with people searching for your services online.

Note: Keep in mind that your customers can also add images to your profile and their reviews. Customers adding photos to their ratings along with written reviews are considered high-quality reviews. Customer- and Google user-uploaded images are still viewable to the public and impact the way new searchers see you. In most cases, they are appropriate, but depending on the nature of those images, you'll be able to flag them should they be offensive or present privacy and legal concerns.

Add Products and Services

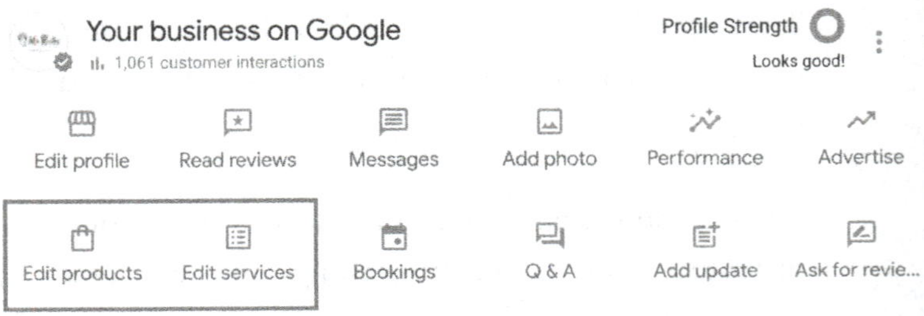

Depending on the type of business you are optimizing a profile for, you may have access to additional features, such as products and services. These categories are determined by your business categories, and some of the information in them may also be generated automatically by Google as a suggested update or changed automatically.

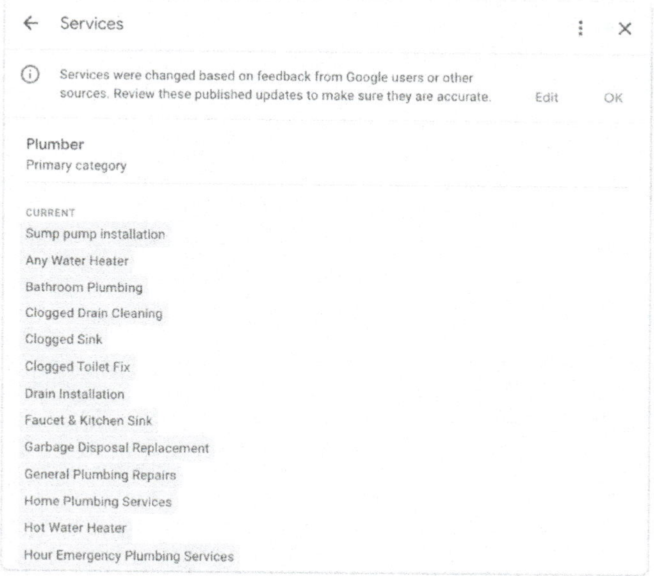

For businesses that offer specific products and services, it's important to fill out these Google Business Profile categories accurately. It plays a major role in determining local search rankings, especially in relation to the relevance of those profiles to online searches. Product descriptions can accommodate up to 1000 characters. Be sure to include the landing page URL with a UTM. On the other hand, service descriptions can only have up to 300 characters.

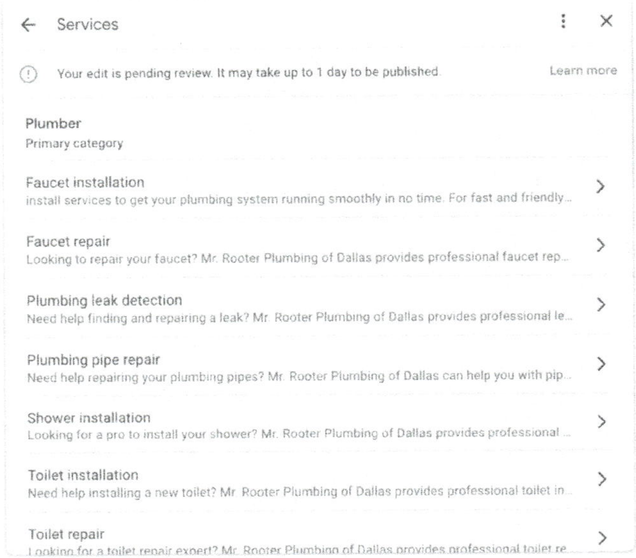

Note: You can change, add and remove products and services as you see fit, but be aware that Google may alter your changes automatically.

Products require an image and have more options for additional details, while services require only a description. You can also add details about the prices of products and services directly to your profile.

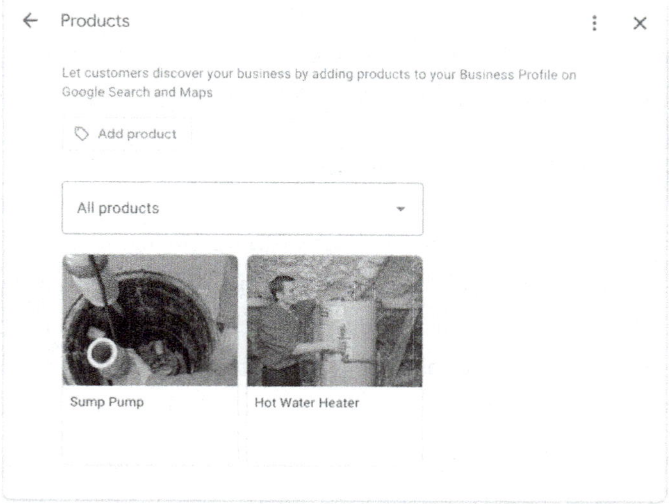

Bookings Section

Adding a bookings tab to your Google Business Profile could facilitate a searcher's efforts, allowing them to make bookings and appointments through your GBP. This is a good method to encourage conversions. There are some handy third-party integration tools available, allowing customers to book a job when it is convenient for them. Ensure that your link includes a UTM to help you identify where the user is from and what they might be looking for.

Google Business Profile Messaging Feature is No More

The Google Business profile messaging feature has

been depreciated. It was underutilized, and owners complained that they received a lot of spam or sales inquiries from this feature.

Check Your Q&A Section

The Q&A section of your Google Business Profile allows people to ask questions and engage with you directly. It can also play a role in boosting user engagement and may help with both relevance and prominence based on what's being asked and how you or other users answer.

Any unanswered questions in your Q&A can have a negative effect on your GBP, so be sure to take the time to answer them. One positive aspect is that past customers who participated in the Q&A will get a notification of new questions, given them the opportunity to respond.

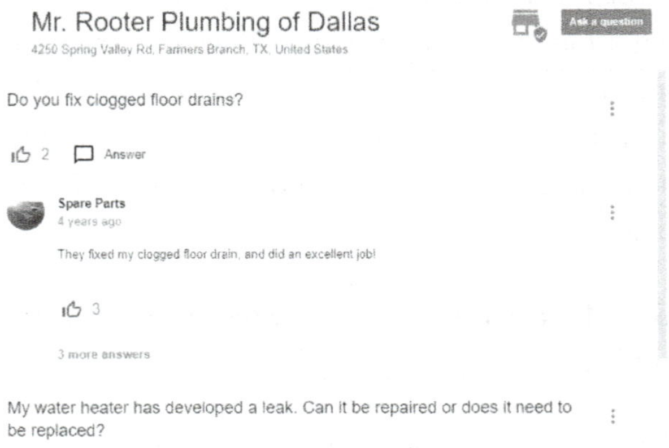

To get the FAQ engagement going, you can create and answer your own questions. This serves a similar function to an FAQ section on your business website. Any essential info you add in an FAQ, such as details about operating procedures or specific offerings, could do well in your Google Business Profile in the form of a Q&A. More importantly, you can add questions that prospective customers ask your CSRs or reception.

Business Attributes and Other Settings

Depending on your primary and secondary categories, your setting may have different options. Review all available options and ensure your profile is accurate and up-to-date. Below is a list of some of the most common options used by home services, but don't worry if you don't see all of these on your profile:

From the business: Use attributes to highlight specific aspects of your business, such as "Women-led" or "Veteran-led."

Offering: You can identify whether you have repair services.

Payments: Indicate the type of payment methods you accept.

Planning: Indicate whether an appointment is required or not.

Service options: Select yes or no based on how you do business and what you offer, i.e.:

- Offers online estimates
- Onsite services available

Be Sure To Follow Google's Guidelines

Google has a specific set of guidelines that business owners must follow when filling out their Google Business Profiles. As long as you represent your business accurately and honestly, it's unlikely that you will find yourself in violation of these guidelines. However, there are some situations where business owners accidentally break one of Google's guidelines, which can result in a suspended listing. Rectifying the issue could cost you valuable time in addition to lost leads and potential job bookings. Ensure that you have read and reviewed Google's guidelines carefully if you are managing it yourself or working with a local SEO company like Digital Shift. Any time you are unsure about what you are doing when filling out your profile, seek out an SEO professional for assistance.

When Should You Hire An SEO Company To Optimize Your Google Business Profile?

A good indicator of when to reach out is when you notice a sharp drop off or spikes in Google Business profile engagement or rankings. For instance, if you notice you're starting to lose jobs to a competitor, they could be starting to outrank you. Or if you or your team are just getting too busy with other work to manage it, that's a good problem to have!

It's unfortunate that some business owners first reach out to an SEO company when they find themselves faced with a suspended Google Business Profile. If your profile has been suspended, there is a specific set of procedures that must be followed to lift the suspension, since Google doesn't provide a definite reason in their communication. Hiring an SEO expert can help you ensure the process runs smoothly. They will help you identify why your profile has been suspended and how to avoid a suspension in the future.

You can also avoid a suspension outright and get fantastic results from your optimization by contacting an SEO company before encountering problems. A well-versed SEO team brings the skill and experience needed to handle Google Business Profile optimization effectively. Ask the company you hire for case studies that have shown proven results, and you will never have to worry about unwanted disruptions again. Be sure to do your due diligence by interviewing multiple SEO agencies to make sure you make an educated decision.

Video Verification is the New Standard

In the past Google was looking for two primary documents with matching information, including the business names and addresses proof of business registration and proof of ongoing business operation. Although having this information up-to-date and available is still important, video verification is the standard for reverifying and opening a new location.

Verifying Google profiles has changed to enforce that everyone is following guidelines and not help mitigate spam listings. In the past you'd be able to request a postcard via mail, enter the code and that was mostly it. If there were any issues, you could send in a couple of pictures of the exterior and interior and proof of business registration and proof of operating at that address. Nowadays the standard is video verification.

Conclusion

You could call the above-outlined strategy SEO GBP, as a good SEO strategy begins with a well-optimized Google Business Profile. Having a transparent profile is crucial if you want to generate organic traffic and achieve positive outcomes.

The essentials you learned in this chapter will go a long way when you apply them now. After all, GBP is a free tool you can use to your advantage.

Now, let's summarize the steps for creating your GBP covered in this chapter:

- Complete all Google Profile sections.
- Enter your accurate business information and complete your business description, optimizing it with keywords relevant to your business.
- Set primary and secondary categories if you offer more than one major service.
- Upload an original, optimized profile logo and cover images. Include images with every service or product that you plan to highlight.
- Upload high-quality videos and photos.
- Engage in customer interaction via Q&A.
- Encourage customers to leave reviews and build a culture with your team around doing so.

- Focus on Google's three main ranking factors: relevance, distance, and prominence. Ensure your services are **relevant** to the local searcher and your business's location is within their **proximity**. You could eventually reach the stage of prominence.

- When optimizing your GBP for success, your business will appear in Google's Search, Maps, Local Finder, and Pack.

CHAPTER 3: HOW TO MAKE USE OF LOCAL CITATIONS TO IMPROVE BUSINESS LISTING MANAGEMENT

In this chapter, we examine:

- Business listing and local citation fundamentals
- Paid and free business listing
- The importance of consistency and regular monitoring and updates
- What to do when moving a business location

When you register your business on paper, you become incorporated with a business number. As the government registers your company immediately, you must do a lot of work before you can make yourself visible and accessible to potential clients. You are now a legal entity with a license and a certificate of incorporation, but where do you go from here?

The answer: You can achieve success by effectively managing local citations and maintaining accurate business listings. Not only do you want to be found at the top of Google's local search engine rankings, but you also want to earn searchers' trust and build credibility for your business.

This chapter will show you how to find local citation opportunities and how to improve your business listing in a crowded and competitive marketplace.

What Is a Local Citation?

A local citation is a reference to your business name, address, phone number, and link in a business directory listing website, such as yelp.ca, yellowpages.ca, or homeadvisor.com. A structured local citation is your complete business name, address, and phone number (NAP data). You may also provide a NAP+W, which includes your website. The consistency of your NAP data is important for SEO purposes and local ranking. Your business information contains local values, which will show up in local business directories, online apps, and social platforms. However, that alone is not enough to generate leads or draw your target audience's attention to your services. You may or may not have an established website. If you don't, it's highly important your citations are accurate, informative, and fully backed by your business listing.

What Is an Unstructured or Partial Citation?

An unstructured or partial citation is a reference to your business information that is outside of the traditional directory listing (structured citations) found on blogs, event listing websites, job websites, newspaper websites, knowledge base websites, government websites, etc. This information helps Google see your business as an entity and consists of some components of the NAP+W information. For instance, it can be just your business name and address listed on another local website as a resource.

What Is the Difference Between Local Citation and Business Listing?

A business listing is a more detailed citation that often also includes your email contact, business hours, directions, an in-depth description of your business, and images. Well-optimized listings will also include service links that provide concise information about what a reader might be looking for. The accuracy of your NAP data makes your business listing more transparent. Plus, the combination of local citation (both structured and unstructured) and business listing also increases your local SEO values.

Why Are Business Listings Important?

Having a strong local citation helps increase your brand's visibility within Google and enables the searcher to find what they are looking for quickly. Combined with useful business listings that contain valuable information, such as visuals, you could outrank other local competitors and get more favorable results. That includes people clicking on your website or visiting your social media platforms for easy-to-consume information or even entertainment.

An optimized business listing also builds Google's trust and proves to potential clients that your reputable business's online presence is well-managed and up-to-date.

Local mentions in the form of structured or unstructured citations and local links are a part of the fundamentals and signals to build credibility and trust in Google's eyes and helps you rank.

PRO TIP: In addition to the top business listing, get listed in directories that are relevant to your industry and geographic area.

Evolution and Adaptation of Other Local Business Platforms

Local business features on Apple and Bing are evolving with more features, and have opportunities for increased user adoption. Apple Business Connect has emerged as a new platform for businesses to optimize their presence on Apple Maps. This is becoming increasingly relevant as more iOS users rely on Apple Maps for local searches. Features include updating links, showcasing photos, and insights on clicks, searches, and other user actions. Optimizing the profiles ensures that the information is accurate and visually appealing to users across Apple Maps, Messages, Wallet, Siri, and other iOS apps.

I'm Relocating My Business: What Do I Do?

Any changes within the business, such as a new address or phone number, must be updated immediately. Ensure you update the information on your website and your Google Business Profile's dashboard by following the verification steps carefully. Remember to also update your NAP on all your social channels and other existing references and publications. Chances are, you will need to update your new business information manually, especially with headers and footers in page content.

Updating NAP data can be a time-consuming process, and you could accidentally create errors such as generating duplicate listings. Be sure to monitor your business listings to avoid this issue.

Ensure you follow guidelines and have your business information, such as insurance certificates and lease agreements, updated and available should anything happen with your Google profile status during the update process.

Moving Your Address & Video Verification

The process for moving and verifying a new profile has changed. The exterior of the business, particularly the signage and entrance, is crucial, especially if you want to have your address visible on Google Maps, which is highly recommended as Google favors and trusts profiles with addresses compared to hidden addresses.

PRO TIP: If you're moving your business, ensure your signage is up and documents updated at your new location before starting the process. This will make the process smoother and avoid potential verification delays.

How To Complete a Local Citation Audit

If you notice errors in your local business listings, you might want to run a local citation audit to clarify any issues. For example, your NAP might be correct in Google Search but incorrect in Bing or Yelp. In this case, a clean-up is necessary.

Luckily, there are some free online tools you can use for the audit, such as Moz Local. Paid tools like BrightLocal can also be used to perform a scan. To find your business online, all you need to do is provide your business information, and your chosen tool will crawl the database of various sites. Most tools are designed to only pull the essential pages, including Google, Yelp, Bing, Facebook, Apple Maps, LinkedIn, and the top listing sites.

If you want to dig deeper into the audit by yourself, you could rely on Google's overall database. In order to do that, you could type in your company name combined with the old address and see what comes up. While MapQuest might have your updated information, Yellow Pages could be outdated. Please note that you could end up with an exhaustive list of outdated information or even duplicate listings, requiring you to manually edit each page. Either way, focus on the essential pages first, followed by local listings in your area and then industry-specific sites.

How To Increase Your Local Citation Opportunities

Local citation building is an important part of your overall local SEO strategy. When done right, you could increase the traffic to your website and improve your ranking in search engines.

- **Claim/create your GBP**: If you haven't already claimed or created your Google Business Profile, do so right away and start optimizing it.

- **Register with paid online directories**: Besides Google, there is a list of local directories and niche sites that are relevant to your business. Once they have verified you, you'll be able to start growing your business in your local area!

- **Consider data aggregators**: This process is similar to what we mentioned previously about performing a local citation audit. Data aggregation summarizes information gathered from major search engines and creates a statistical analysis. This way, you'll be able to rectify any errors. It can help you stay organized because you'll have an overview of your own data. Should any changes occur, you will know immediately where you need to perform updates.

- **Monitor and be aware of Google updates**: Many small updates happen throughout the year and are often not announced, but Google will usually announce core updates. Updates can affect your local citation; there could be a new feature added, a feature removed or an update to Google's guidelines. Many business owners can fall behind when actively focusing on growing their business and serving customers. Regularly monitoring your local rankings and citations helps you stay on track and avoid a potential downfall.

PRO TIP: Join a newsletter, watch for updates from Google Search Liaison on X, or check https://status.search.google.com/summary for updates and information.

- **Encourage customer reviews**: Google reviews are a huge part of your local reputation, and one of the first things searchers will notice are star ratings and the number of reviews. Also, the reviews themselves can contain useful information like pictures and keywords that reflect the type of work your business does. These reviews help Google better understand the relationship between your listing and what you do. As a result, your local business can rank better in local search results.

How To Improve Your Google Business Listing

Once you have claimed your Google Business Profile and confirmed your business information, including the NAP, is accurate, you want to ensure the details in your business listing are also accurate. An actively managed business listing can provide you with a wide range of possibilities.

To improve your Google Business listings' rankings on Maps, you should:

- Be **proactive** when maintaining your local citation accuracy.

- Expand on your business description with SEO-optimized **texts**, **images**, and **videos** in the form of a slideshow. Additionally, you can include relevant secondary categories with high-ranking keywords. But be sure to fill any gaps in your business listing.

- Increase **customer engagement** by replying to questions promptly, whether it's in the FAQ section, direct Google messages, or replying to their reviews. Also, pay attention to how users interact with your social media content, as that can affect how they interact with your business listing.

- Encourage your employees to ask the customer for a **Google review** once a service has been completed. Keep in mind that it should be a simple process for your client, such as receiving a link or a QR code that takes them straight to the review box. Helpful reviews contain relevant keywords that can complement your business listing description and, thus, help you rank higher.

- Use **Google Search Console** to check your website's indexing status. The Index Coverage report is a valuable tool for webmasters and SEO professionals to identify and address issues that may affect a website's visibility in Google's search results.

- **Log in to your Google Business Profile** often to check for suggested updates or new features, even if there are no new reviews or questions. Also, update your business listing when necessary, such as uploading new photos or highlighting popular or seasonal services.

Invest In Paid Online Directory Listings To Stand Out With Your Local Citation and Business Listings!

Google isn't all that matters for local businesses. Once you have a fully optimized website and strong local citations, expand on your internet marketing strategy by engaging with local online directories. These are effective marketing platforms to help you gain more exposure.

What Are Paid Online Directory Listings?

Paid online directories charge your business either a one-time or recurring fee to list your business information. There are similar options to non-paid directory listings, but they can be seen as more credible because they help filter out fake or spam listings by charging a fee. These are designed to give your business listing credibility in addition to what Google already provides.

That said, every paid online directory operates differently. Some are free to register but charge an advertising fee. Whereas others charge a monthly or yearly subscription fee. Depending on your niche and location, make sure you sign up with a citation site that is relevant to your type of business. Check if your competitors are listed and whether they get a lot of local customer engagement. If so, you can get there too by identifying any keyword research gaps, and eventually, you'll be able to outrank them.

The most popular business directory listing websites:

- Yelp
- Yellow Pages
- Foursquare
- BBB
- Angi
- HomeAdvisor
- Bing Places
- Apple Maps
- MapQuest

Businesses have the ability to claim, or create, business listings in many different places; however, doing so requires dedication that includes data management and regular user interactions.

It's highly recommended that you focus on fully optimizing your Google Business Profile first when working on your lead generation and marketing strategies. You will always have time to look at each citation site in more detail once you get the ball rolling. Just remember that each citation site benefits a specific industry more than others. For example, Yelp is for all services, whereas Angi primarily reviews home service providers.

How Do Paid Online Directory Listings Make Your Business Stand Out?

Ultimately, citation sites are designed to help online searchers instantly identify and learn more about a local business. As a result, this helps businesses develop brand awareness faster too. When signing up with a paid online directory, you often need to verify business ownership through a verification process, most commonly using the business phone number. For example, a code will be provided to you via a robocall from the website directory to your business number that you enter to verify that you have access to the phone number of your business on their site. Once you have passed it, you are instantly recognized as a registered business, and this helps you build credibility and boost your Google Business listings' visibility.

Let's switch gears and spend some time getting to know more about pay-per-lead services, which are an important part of business visibility.

What Are Pay-Per-Lead Services?

Essentially, you, the advertiser, pay an affiliate a commission for any leads they manage to generate for you. A lead is not yet a customer, but you can measure how close they are to becoming one. When using pay-per-lead services, you must be diligent and always follow up with your potential leads. Once you have a lead, you will only have limited time to convert them into a paying customer. While you have their attention, ask them how they are doing. Then, highlight their struggles and courteously offer to eliminate their problems with your services by including exclusive special offers.

If you don't keep up with your leads, you could throw away a lot of money. Overall, pay-per-lead is not a sustainable strategy for long-term success, but it can be useful for campaigns or promotional purposes.

Conclusion

Your GBP, local citation, and business listing are for more than just providing basic information to online searchers. These platforms, especially GBP, allow users to engage with local businesses. They include many websites with features visible to the public directly on Google, without the need to visit the website. This provides many growth opportunities as long as you remain proactive and engage with your potential customers' queries.

To be successful online:

- Ensure you have a well-optimized GBP before you invest time and money in business directories.

- Local citations and business listings require regular upkeep to ensure that local values are maintained and eventually, enhanced.

- Make use of tools to run local citation (business listings) audits if you detect any errors.

- Stay proactive and engage in customer queries and social interactions.

- Pay-per-leads and other marketing strategies can be useful when running campaigns and promotions.

- Check where your competitions are at and plan a strategy to do better.

CHAPTER 4: WHAT ARE THE BEST STRATEGIES FOR EFFECTIVE GOOGLE BUSINESS PROFILE MANAGEMENT?

In this chapter, we cover:

- Optimizing your profile to maximize visibility online
- Maintaining prominence and relevance
- Increasing engagement with potential customers
- Encouraging and managing reviews
- Regular posts and updates

As a local business, you have a Google Business Profile (GBP) that helps you manage your online presence so local customers can easily find you. But having a GBP is more than just stating that your business exists. It also serves the important purpose of ensuring that all of your business's essential details are available at a glance. There are many useful and effective ways of using your GBP to improve your local SEO and drive sales. From increasing customer engagement to boosting your brand's reputation, your Google Business Profile is the first impression searchers get. This makes it incredibly important to have an effective strategy that manages it in the best possible way.

The Goals of GBP Management

Before mapping out your SEO strategy, it is essential that you set goals for GBP management. It is a time-consuming process, as the primary goal is to get customer engagement in the form of reviews or Q&As. As time goes on, your business will grow, and more and more online participants will engage and use the available information.

However, setting goals involves engaging with your audience and answering their questions quickly before they change their minds and look elsewhere. By delivering immediately and providing accurate information, you are more likely to succeed in terms of converting online searchers into customers. Proper GBP management will help you meet many company goals.

Increasing Engagement

What ingredients do you need to have a satisfied customer? The answer in your case would be the combination of quality workmanship and superior customer service. But you don't let a happy customer go after a well-done job. Instead, you want to utilize a customer engagement strategy to help build a genuine connection with them. You can do this by seeking feedback through different communication channels, such as social media, Google reviews, emails, phone calls, and more. The key to customer engagement is to remain consistent, as reviews and social posts are dated. The fresher the content, the better the chances for customer engagement content to rank high in search engines.

Reputation and Brand Management

A properly managed GBP can greatly enhance the reputation of your local business. With accurate information and plenty of positive customer feedback, you'll create brand awareness. Locals are drawn to your products and services, and therefore, you can position your brand in the right place to target your desired customers.

Maintaining Prominence and Relevance

Prominence is about how well your business is known in your local community. Not every business is locally famous, but the good news is that you don't have to be. Being relevant to your community is more significant than fame, as it means that your local customers need you. Perhaps the local home services you provide are of seasonal significance. In that case, you want to get the ball rolling by keeping your GBP up-to-date and relevant. It's never too late to acquire more prominence in your area, and your GBP can help you achieve that.

The Goals of Managing a Google Business Profile are to:

1. **Improve visibility**: By managing your Google Business Profile, you can ensure that accurate and up-to-date information about your business is displayed in search results, Google Maps, and other Google services. This will increase your business's visibility and make it easier for potential customers to find you.

2. **Enhance credibility**: A well-maintained Google Business Profile will enhance your credibility with potential customers. It demonstrates that you take your business seriously and that you care about providing accurate information to your customers.

3. **Engage with customers**: Managing your Google Business Profile also helps you engage with customers. It enables you to respond directly to customer reviews, answer questions, and post updates about your business. This allows you to build

relationships with customers and increase their loyalty to your business.

4. **Monitor performance**: By monitoring your Google Business Profile, you can track key metrics, including the number of views, clicks, and calls that your business receives. This will help you understand how customers are finding and interacting with your business and identify areas for improvement.

Setting goals for your Google Business Profile management will improve your business's online presence and build credibility with local customers. Engage with them in a meaningful way, and you will reap the benefits later on.

Managing Your Google Reviews

Reviews matter—a lot! According to the Local Consumer Review Survey conducted by BrightLocal, 98% of people read online reviews for local businesses, and 76% read reviews regularly. Prospects read Google reviews prior to deciding on a service or purchase. Keeping up with your customer review management requires tact and dedication. Whether you get positive or negative reviews, your engagement proves to your community that you care about customer experience and feedback. Though it doesn't mean you need to reply to every single review, you want to make sure your overall customer sentiment analysis is positive. There are many small details to keep in mind when managing your Google reviews.

What's Important For Google Reviews?

- **Total Number of Reviews**: The higher the number of reviews, the more customer engagement you can expect.

- **Quality of Reviews**: Often, online searchers want to learn directly from other customers about their experience with a local business. To ensure positive customer engagement, you want to reply to client reviews, no matter if they are bad or good. This way, new readers will learn more about how you treat your customers.

- **Diversity**: The quantity and diversity of reviews account for over 15% of what's required to appear in local searches, so those factors do have an impact on your SEO. However, keep in mind that the details in your GBP, such as your name, address, and phone number (NAP), already have a high ranking factor.

- **Frequency**: Review diversity also marks how fast and how frequently you get reviews. Plus, you might have received company reviews on a third-party website that has a high domain authority. In that case, it will greatly influence your local rankings.

When managing your Google reviews, remember that various factors play a role in how Google perceives the review content. There's more to consider besides a website's content quality, keyword usage, site speed, and signals from local links. A customer's review may also be helpful to prospective customers and Google if it contains significant proof relevant to your business and services in the form of photos and written review details.

Responding to Customer Reviews

Check your business's review section and respond to any new reviews that have been left. This shows that not only do you care about your customers, but also that you are actively engaging with them.

Responding to Positive Reviews

Replying to positive reviews is crucial in terms of building strong relationships with your clients. It shows that you deeply care about their experience and you want to ensure they will return or even recommend your business to friends and acquaintances. Moreover, you want to attract new potential clients.

Responding to positive reviews on Google is important for several reasons:

1. **Builds a positive reputation**: Responding to positive reviews helps to reinforce the positive image of your business. It shows that you appreciate and value your customers and that you take the time to read and respond to their feedback.

2. **Encourages more positive reviews**: When you respond to positive reviews, it encourages other customers to leave positive reviews as well. This can help to build a cycle of positive reviews that can benefit your business.

3. **Increases customer loyalty**: When you respond to positive reviews, it shows customers that you are committed to providing excellent service. This will help increase customer loyalty and encourage repeat business in the future.

4. **Provides valuable feedback**: Positive reviews can provide valuable feedback on what customers like about your business. Responding to these reviews helps you identify areas of your business that are working well so that you can continue to build on them.

Overall, responding to positive reviews on Google is an integral part of building a positive online reputation. It strengthens relationships with your clients while attracting new ones.

Responding to Negative Reviews

It is also important to respond to negative reviews on Google because it shows that you care about your customers and their experience with your business. Responding to negative reviews can also help:

1. **Address the customer's concerns**: By responding to a negative review, you can acknowledge the customer's concerns and offer a solution or an explanation.

2. **Improve your business**: Negative reviews can provide valuable feedback that can help you improve your business, products, or services. By responding to negative reviews, you can show that you are actively working to address the issues that your customers have raised.

3. **Build trust and credibility**: When potential customers see that you are actively engaging with your customers and addressing their concerns, they are more likely to trust and choose your business over competitors.

4. **Increase customer loyalty**: Responding to negative reviews shows that you value your customers and their opinions. It shows that you genuinely care about their negative experience and that you're determined to do better. This can lead to increased customer loyalty and repeat business.

When responding to negative customer reviews, take the conversation offline to connect with them directly instead of trying to resolve the issues in public on the Google review feature.

Overall, responding to negative reviews on Google is an important part of managing your online reputation and building a positive relationship with your customers.

How Do You Get More Google Reviews?

Time is valuable, and not everyone is willing to spare two or five minutes to write a review—unless they're getting something out of it. Despite providing exceptional service, the magical feedback of a happy customer can easily go unwritten or untold if you let it slip through your fingers.

Luckily, there are ways to prevent this from happening.

Train Your Team to Ask Customers

Your employees are hardworking and courteous by nature, and, like you, they want the business to thrive and expand. Besides providing excellent customer service and craftsmanship, encourage them to go the extra mile and humbly ask customers for feedback on Google. The last thing your customer wants is to sit in front of a computer and type in your business name. Fortunately, there are faster and more effective ways.

Make It Easy!

Provide a direct link to your Google Business Profile and encourage customers to leave a review by giving them clear instructions on how to do so. Effective options include asking before leaving the home after the service is completed and providing a QR code to scan, texting the clients, calling, and emailing. Be sure to also share the link on your social channels.

Create a Review Landing Page

Create a review page on your website. You can ask your franchisee marketing department or developer or use a third-party app or widget on your website yourself. This not only allows you to showcase your reviews but also to collect new ones. So all your customers have to do is click the link, provide feedback, and send it your way.

Distribute Review Cards and QR Codes

QR codes have revolutionized the way we access and provide information. All you need is your GBP's review share link and a QR code generator. Next, you can customize the code the way you want and even add a friendly message thanking your customer for their business.

If you're not already asking before leaving their home, consider leaving a review card with the client right after a service. Or depending on how you collect a payment, print QR codes directly onto your receipts.

Develop Employee Review Incentives

We have all been there—missing out on asking the ideal customer for a Google review. To prevent this from happening, you can provide incentives to your employees. It's an enticing way of motivating them to collect customer feedback and help your business grow. Reward the team member who has collected the most reviews of the month to encourage others to compete for the following month. Ensure you follow Google's policies and guidelines for reviews and do not provide monetary incentives to customers for leaving reviews. Violating these policies can result in consequences such as the removal of reviews or possible suspension of your Google listing.

Follow Up With Recent Customers via Email and Phone

By following up with your client, you make the whole customer service package complete. You can give your clients a brief call to ensure they are truly satisfied with your service and also encourage them to leave you a positive review.

Note: You might also want to advise your customers to follow Google review guidelines in case they are not familiar with them.

Utilize Social Media

Create and share information like reviews and customer feedback on Google and other social media channels. It's a good method of increasing your business's success and creating brand awareness. Most social channels, like Facebook, have review features, and they are helpful but not as powerful as Google reviews when it comes to increasing map rankings.

Update Your Business Information

Did you move your business or change your contact information? If so, be sure to update your office hours, address, phone number, and other business information where applicable. This is important for ensuring that customers can find and reach you.

Uploading New Photos and Videos

When learning about a local business, most people like to see visuals rather than plain text. It gives them the opportunity to learn who you are, what you do, and where you provide services. More importantly, photographs and videos should be category-specific to help searchers differentiate your type of business.

Technical optimization here includes using geotagged images and making sure they are localized with GPS coordinates of the location. This way, they are relevant to the area you're targeting. You also want to make sure that you use original yet professional photographs, rather than stock images, for your GBP.

Managing Your Products and Services

Ensure that the products and services advertised are accurate so you don't confuse your potential customers. Remove any services you don't wish to promote and highlight those that are relevant to the current season, especially if you focus on different services in spring/summer and fall/winter. It also helps to research services similar to yours and see what is currently trending.

Watch Out for These Updates and Changes to Your Profile:

1. **Automatic updates from Google**: With Google's ever-changing algorithms, your GBP's style and format could also change on a periodic basis. There may be a new section or feature that requires your attention. The sooner you update it, the sooner Google will be able to use this piece of information to help you rank. While Google applies small updates to its algorithms all the time, it's the major updates you especially want to watch out for. Sometimes there is zero notice when an update comes out, so it's a good idea to subscribe to a newsletter from a trusted source, like Digital Shift, to keep you informed and help you prepare.

2. **User-suggested updates**: Users (competitors included) have the opportunity to suggest edits and updates to your GBP. It is recommended that you check these immediately in your dashboard and either accept or reject them. Unauthorized suggestions still matter to local businesses. They help you evaluate user experience, track where your traffic comes from, and can potentially improve your ranking.

Adding Descriptions for New Services and Products

Are you promoting a new service or product? If so, add a detailed yet precise description of it and remember to expand on the value it will bring to your customers. Ensure you use all the features and write unique descriptions for each of your services. A Google post with a limited-time offer or promotion can also help drive sales and increase your conversion rate.

PRO TIP: If you go to your services, you might see messages like "Services were changed based on feedback from Google users or other sources. Review these published updates to make sure they are accurate." This means it's time to review your details.

Engage with Potential Customers

If customers have questions or comments on your profile, respond to them in a timely and professional manner. This can help build trust and rapport with potential clients and also help drive more business to your company. Timely customer engagement is important whether they reach out to you via your website's contact form, social media, or business phone.

Managing Your Google Business Q&A Section

Besides having contact information available, a

Q&A section is a convenient way for potential customers to find the immediate answer they are looking for. It saves them time from having to call or email.

Responding to Questions From Prospective Clients

Depending on your specific business niche, there is always a wide range of questions that potential clients may ask. It could be about the product or service itself, or they want to know more about the process. The sooner you reply to their queries, the more likely they will be to choose your service.

Adding Your Own FAQs

As described in the previous chapter about setting up your GBP, your Google Business Profile allows you to create your own FAQs (Frequently Asked Questions). We recommend gathering a list of top client questions and picking the most relevant ones for your GBP's FAQ section. This way, you can provide answers online before new clients ask them again. Some questions may be tricky to answer (i.e., cost-related questions), so it's best to encourage searchers to call to tell you about the situation and job requirements.

FAQs can be effective at answering questions of whether you service a particular area or provide a specific type of service. For instance, if your customer service reps get calls frequently about a service you don't offer, you can answer this question in your FAQs to help filter out these types of phone calls from reaching your business.

Managing Your Google Business Posts

Google Business Posts are a fantastic way to connect with existing customers and attract new ones. They work similarly to social media and allow you to share a wide array of enticing content about the areas you serve, the service you provide, as well as other helpful information to homeowners.

Review and use all the latest posting features. Your posts can include text, images, and even call-to-action buttons, such as "Learn More," "Book," or "Call Now."

What Should You Post to Your Google Business Profile?

We recommend posting promotional content, offers, announcements, photographs, videos, and much more. Keeping your profile fresh and engaging by posting new content and updates on your Google Business Profile regularly. Performing these activities and getting engagement from prospective customers can also help increase your online credibility and influence your position on Google Maps.

How Can You Stay Consistent With Posting?

The best way to stay on top of your posts is to plan ahead and be proactive when engaging with your followers. People love visuals, which include photographs and videos. There is a reason why social media has ascended to the marketing throne as the "new word of mouth." It is engaging, which makes it a useful tool for conversion. But how do you stay consistent with posting? Planning your social posts can easily be managed by keeping an organized content calendar.

Some different types of posts and ideas to include in your content calendar are:

- Information/blogs
- Areas served
- Services
- Customer reviews
- Fun facts/humor
- Events, promotions, and coupons
- Showcase your work with photos of completed work, such as before and after images
- You and your team

Monitor Your Insights

Google provides insights into how many people are viewing your profile and engaging with your content. Evaluate these insights and use them to make data-driven decisions about your Google Business Profile.

The GBP click-to-call metric is one of the most important ones to keep an eye out for, so ensure that you include this call to action for relevant posts to help increase activity.

By consistently updating and maintaining your Google Business Profile, you'll help your business stand out online, attract more customers and increase your conversion rate.

Conclusion

A well-managed GBP allows you to stay on track of its overall performance. It involves a lot of interaction with online searchers, where timeliness plays an important role. To summarize this chapter, here's why Google Business Profile Management is essential to your business:

- Enhances brand awareness and reputation, which means your GBP is relevant and prominent within your targeted area.

- Increases customer interaction, leading to a greater potential for conversions. This is especially true if your service is of seasonal significance.

- Helps you keep track of customer reviews and

Google messages. As long as you reply in a timely manner, you can expect positive results.

The more you encourage customers to leave reviews, the more attention you will draw in your local area. Treat your GBP similarly to your social channels and post content that is relevant and enticing. When you hire an experienced SEO team, they will know the significance of creating consistent content to drive engagement on your profile and positively influence your calls, leads, and job bookings.

CHAPTER 5: WHAT IS WEBSITE OPTIMIZATION, AND WHY IS IT IMPORTANT?

In this chapter, you'll learn about the following:

- Significance of the user experience
- The importance of your website structure and sitemap
- What structured data (schema data) does
- Webpage best practices
- Difference between on-page SEO and off-page SEO

It is easy to create a website nowadays thanks to user-friendly website builders that facilitate the process. But despite this convenience, you're likely experiencing a low engagement rate (the updated term for Google Analytics 4) or high bounce rate (the Universal Analytics or Google Analytics 3 term that you are likely used to hearing about)—one of the major factors, in addition to the audience and offer, when trying to convert website visitors into customers. This is where website optimization comes in to improve user experience and help you meet your business goals.

While it's great to set business goals for increasing your conversion rate, you must take some essential technical steps toward improving your website performance. From usability and loading time to mobile-friendly designs, in this chapter, we'll see what website optimization is all about and why it is important.

Understanding Website Design

First, you need to understand the design you choose, or the one provided by your franchisor, for your website. There is a wide variety of designs and functionalities to suit different types of businesses. For example, if your website is meant to convert, you want your company logo to appear in the top left corner of the page, whereas your phone number should be on the right. On the main page, you should include professional photographs, main navigation, a small blurb, and a clear CTA (Call to Action).

To help maximize prospective website visitors turning into paying customers, it's also extremely important to have your phone number clearly listed, usually in the top right-hand corner of your website, or to have a click-to-call button on your mobile website.

But that's not everything. Sizing and positioning are imperative in a well-constructed design and layout because they can determine the number of conversions you get. After all, users like well-curated content and a main page that is easy to navigate. To further experiment with designs, you can run tests with A/B testing that allows you to put up two design versions and see which one performs best.

Website designs are built using different formats, and they can get very technical depending on which one you choose.

Next, we'll walk you through the details of a few common website formats to showcase their differences.

Common Website Formats

- **HTML:** Short for HyperText Markup Language, HTML is the forerunner of website creation that dates back to the early 1990s. An HTML page is basically a building block that you can incorporate into a website. It's a coded document that is displayed in a browser and can hyperlink multiple pages together.

- **Templates/Site Builders**: A website builder software or platform enables you to create a website without coding knowledge. Some are extremely user-friendly, even for those with less experience creating websites. However, they are more expensive than other platforms.

- **CMS Systems**: Content Management Systems (CMS) are also very popular and straightforward. They are ideal for people who regularly post new content and collaborate with others. CMS is convenient and easy to use for home service businesses, offering powerful features, such as plugins and other add-ons.

Benefits of Content Management Systems

Cost-Effective: Content Management Systems (CMS) systems like WordPress, one of the most popular platforms on the web, are fairly cost-effective compared to site builders that charge a high price for annual subscriptions.

Scalability: As CMS are user-friendly and easy to handle, they encourage you to post content regularly. While doing so, you maintain brand consistency and increase scalability without increasing costs. Enterprise systems like CrownPeak allow for scalability, data integration, and more.

SEO-Friendly: Whether you need to optimize a URL, meta title, or header, CMS allows you to do that with ease. Additionally, you can make use of their plugin tools to optimize your site further.

User Access Management: Although several people have login access, you can determine who gets access to features, what actions they perform and areas of the site they can use. You can also set roles to work with your business workflow and needs.

Simple to Use: CMS are generally beginner-friendly and easy to learn. They can be used in a wide range of capabilities, whether you want to make small edits or more advanced ones (which may require some HTML, PHP, or JavaScript coding knowledge). Updating existing content or adding new pages and blogs is relatively straightforward on most platforms. They also provide a great degree of flexibility without having to use a coder or developer for most updates and changes.

Search Engine Friendly: Most content management systems are optimally structured or can be enhanced through the use of best practices and plugins for SEO. Built-in features allow you to create content and link between pages following technical SEO best practices. This makes CMS search engine friendly by default or with a few tweaks.

Built-in Blogging: You have the flexibility to create useful and helpful content rather easily using built-in blogging templates, and you can structure blogs further into locations or categories depending on your business and niche.

Plugins: Most content management systems allow integration or plugins to help with specific functions. For instance, you can get various plugins to help you reach your goals, such as SEO plugins or integrate social sharing. Some even provide built-in keyword analysis and allow you to add more information besides the metadata.

Do You Need a Mobile-Friendly Website?

The short answer is yes. Your website needs to be fast and offer a flawless user experience on mobile devices.

More than 50% of web visits are conducted via mobile when compared to desktop. Given this statistic, it is crucial for web designers to create mobile-friendly websites for smaller screens. With improved navigation, optimized web speed, and compressed images, they help deliver a great user experience.

While the desktop version of your websites with a comprehensive horizontal navigation bar can also have easily accessible sub-categories, they still need to be accessible for mobile users. When converting from desktop to mobile, horizontal navigation menus are typically minimized into a dropdown menu (or hamburger navigation menu). That's why it is important that you design for every screen size, including tablets.

There is something specialists call the three-click rule, which means your website should be so well-optimized that it shouldn't take the searcher more than three clicks to get where they want to go. Therefore, when optimizing your website for a mobile device, only keep important information accessible and visible.

Why Should Your Website Be Localized?

Once you have mastered the technical aspects of website building, it is time to focus on localization. This is a crucial step toward website optimization and local SEO and a huge part of your content marketing journey. Localized information on your website assists the search engine in understanding who you are targeting and where your customers are located. It also generates a mutual understanding between you and your local community and can establish trust in your company.

By proving to Google who your target audience is, you will automatically improve your brand image. In Google's eyes, you are adapting to the distinctiveness of your audience. This is proof that you are a part of that community and want to deliver value to make a difference. Localized websites enable Google to pull your data and match them with their user data.

What Should a Website Look Like?

As a home service business that has lots of stories to tell and services to offer, you want to ensure that your website looks neat and delivers a high level of professionalism. Your level of expertise and trustworthiness should be backed by professional photographs, business accreditation, awards, and badges.

But where do you begin?

Branding Colors

Branding is important. If you don't have this established already, start by identifying the distinctive colors that align with your company's brand. Do you have an existing logo? Do your staff members wear a company uniform? Create a website with your company's branding colors in mind, as it will help you stand out. While color psychology plays a huge role in determining human mood and behavior, it also reflects one's intentions and personality. Consider a color palette that best describes your business identity.

Important Sections:

We briefly discussed the main page of your website, but let's circle back to look at its essentials. Here's a breakdown of what should be included:

Home Page: Your homepage is the first thing a visitor sees when they arrive at your website. This is where the overall design, layout, and structure of your website will strike their eyes. This is the first impression they get from your company website.

About Us: When customers hire your home service company, they want to know who you are and what you have successfully accomplished in the past. The "about us" page is a part of your brand and is designed to build trust. Staff photographs, names, and background stories deliver transparency, which is important for relationship building and trust.

Why Us: One question that will cross your potential customers' minds is why they should choose your business instead of the competition. Here's where you highlight the benefits they will get when they choose your service. Communicate your company's core values and how your craftsmanship and customer service are like no other. Mention service guarantees and add a link to your reviews and testimonials.

Guarantee: Some brands prefer dedicating a separate page to guarantees and warranties. This makes sense when you deal with a number of parts that have different warranties. Furthermore, you want to restore your customers' peace of mind by offering a labor warranty in case something doesn't meet their expectations.

Services: A menu with a comprehensive list of services offered will highlight your level of expertise and what you do. Expanding on each service by creating individual service pages will help your visitors find specific information as well as influence higher rankings on Google.

Service Area: A localized website helps Google match you with relevant users. Besides the main area you serve, mention surrounding areas, towns, and zip codes that are within your proximity. Or embed a Google Map in your website, including areas that you serve. Creating "areas served" or "geo pages" can help visitors find solutions to more specific search queries users are searching for. Perhaps there's a common issue with a home in the area because of the climate or its age that your technicians are very knowledgeable and experienced in fixing.

Specials and Coupons: Whether you already have loyal customers on an email list or service plan or want to offer new customers a good first-time service deal, coupons and special offers can be a strategy you choose to use for conversion and retention of customers.

Reviews and Testimonials: Having a review presented on your website in a list or "slider" on your website showcasing testimonials helps increase your company's credibility. Well-established websites that have strong domain authority often include a link to local Google reviews.

Image Showcase: High-quality web images are pivotal for home service businesses. Not only should photographs be clear and well-lit, but they must also be formatted, sized, localized, and optimized. Using original images that are specific to your location enhances the authenticity of your brand and can help prospective customers see that you have experience in completing similar projects—especially if you showcase before and after images.

Blog: The blog section is where you inform, educate or entertain your readers. It can include helpful content such as maintenance tips, resources, checklists, home improvement ideas, DIY tips, how-to guides, the latest trends within your industry, or the top ten tips and tricks that only home service providers know. Blogs enable you to post fresh content regularly, as there is always something new and exciting to write about in your industry. It's an effective form of content creation that will help you rank in the local search engine, especially if it's helpful for homeowners, not to mention generate leads and cultivate an online community on your social platforms.

Contact Us: You put yourself out there to be seen. Most of all, you want potential customers to reach out and book your service. Not everyone has the time to shop around, so they seek a phone number they can call to get an immediate response to their queries. By proving to your potential customers that you have a quick response time, they will be more likely to choose your service. On your Contact Us page, in addition to other areas of your website, include a contact form that's easy to use and understand for visitors. As a rule of thumb, the shorter the form with less personal information, the higher the conversion. A simple form that asks for the name, email, phone number, postal code/zip, and a message should get you enough details and doesn't compromise your form conversion rate. If you have multiple steps with more information, the lead quality will increase, but it usually results in lower lead volume. Test your lead forms to ensure that no technical issues prevent you or your prospective customer from receiving information or updates from you.

Live Chat: Live chats or chatbots are useful and effective, but they can also be a nuisance to some people. It's best not to have CTA pop-ups or chatbot notifications jump the screen as the user lands on your page right away. Check your Google Analytics to evaluate when and what works, as you can delay pop-ups or even create an exit pop-up that can detect that the user is about to leave the browser.

How Should A Web Page Be Organized?

Besides easy-to-read content, visual hierarchies, user-friendly navigation, and a clutter-free design, it's important to centralize a core message that communicates directly with your audience. While these are the most important aspects of main pages or landing pages, you need to be careful with how you structure them.

Here are some ideas for organizing your webpage:

- **Compelling headline**: Start with a compelling headline followed by a sub-headline and a call-to-action button or a lead capture form. The latter will depend on how you generate leads. Some companies prefer to collect names and contact details so they have a list of prospects to whom they can propose their value.

- **Deliver your message**: To avoid overwhelming the reader, communicate one clear message at the top and state your value proposition there. Then, expand on the benefits below as the reader scrolls down by using bullet points. Keep your content sharp and concise.

- **Highlight popular services**: Users might be interested in your top services that not every home service provider offers or your availability (i.e., 24-hour emergency services).

- **Position captivating images**: Impactful images help place the user in a spot they want to be once they have hired your services. The image could be centered or aligned to the right or left.

- **Integrate social media**: Website integration helps you better measure the effectiveness of your marketing campaigns and keep track of conversions. You'll also encourage customer interaction by embedding your social feed to your website. Also, consider including a signup form and a search bar to increase the chances of conversions and help users find what they are looking for.

- **Include trust icons**: Trust badges highlight any awards and certifications that your company was granted. Many trusted, non-profit organizations (i.e., Consumer Choice

Award, BBB - Better Business Bureau, etc.) are committed to helping consumers choose the best services. Trust icons help establish trust and brand awareness.

- **Add phone number**: Include your company's phone number in the top right corner where it is clearly visible. It should be easily found and can be visually appealing when adjacent to your company logo, which is embedded in the top left corner. Your business contact information, such as your address, can be placed near the bottom of the page with the quick links in the footer area.

PRO TIP: Make it easy for prospective customers to click and call you from the mobile version of your website to increase conversion rates.

- **Payment information**: Share with users the forms of payment that you accept at the bottom of the page.

- **Privacy policy link**: Privacy and other types of disclaimers also fit best at the bottom of the page.

Why Do Layouts Need to Be User-Friendly?

A well-structured layout ensures a good user experience. Keep in mind that you'll have desktop, tablet, and mobile users. Disorganized content can be confusing for users, as well as search engines, to navigate, which can trigger them to leave. This is especially true for mobile users who rely on clarity and accessibility to help them find the most relevant content.

What is Technical SEO?

Technical SEO is the process of website and server optimization. It's designed to help search engines crawl and index pages more effectively. This is where Google Search Console comes in to help you monitor, maintain and troubleshoot your website's presence in the search results. You may occasionally get a notification about crawl errors that need to be corrected to avoid a decrease in search performance.

The technical side of SEO ensures that your website's coding is clean and well-formatted. Every website optimization process and general SEO strategy should include technical SEO. So rather than just worrying about on-page SEO strategies and keyword density, keep in mind that technical SEO is also a high priority.

What is Page Experience, and How Does It Affect SEO?

Page experience refers to user experience, and Google has a way of measuring experience metrics for each website and its individual URLs. Google's evaluation will determine how well you rank in the search results.

This makes it crucial that your website is technically optimized so it effectively supports user experience. If your website is technically optimized, its visibility in searches will increase.

Page experience has become a more significant Google Search ranking factor. When measuring and collecting user experience data, Google examines page load times and mobile friendliness. In short, your SEO strategy also relies on a technically optimized website that delivers an exceptional page experience.

How Does Page Speed Affect SEO?

Page speed is an essential aspect of page experience and serves as a significant factor in determining quality websites and rankings. If your page is overwhelmed with bad file types or heavy images, the long loading time will only frustrate users, triggering them to leave. If your page has an increased bounce rate, it indicates poor performance and may not help you rank well.

What Role Does Site Structure Play in SEO, and How Should It Be Optimized for Both Google and Users?

Site structure refers to how your website's content is organized. The act of organizing your website in an easy-to-understand and logical manner is an essential aspect of site structure. Your website structure will influence your navigation, and this is also where you decide on the placement of the navigation bar, internal links, and breadcrumbs. Breadcrumbs are often referred to as a trail or path that helps your visitors orientate on your website. The links to higher-level pages they visited will be shown, allowing them to return to them in just one click and improving the user experience.

A well-organized site structure plays a huge role in user experience and, therefore, in SEO as well.

Excellent site structure serves as a guide for Google because it crawls webpages by following and examining internal and external links. When Google sees coherence, your site structure will ultimately help you rank in search engines.

Optimizing your site structure for SEO purposes may include updating outdated content, reworking your categories, and improving your internal links.

How Do You Review Your XML Sitemap and Robots.txt Files?

Robots.txt and Sitemap.xml are essential files for crawling and indexing. They help search engines better understand your website and its content and structure. These files are important because bots can scan and rank your pages; moreover, they're able to detect if any page is showing issues. If you have a site issue, Google Search Console will send you a notification detailing the crawling or indexing issues.

The Robots file is placed on the root of the domain. To review your file, visit:

https://www.example.com/**robots.txt**

You should be able to find your primary Sitemap in the robots.txt file. It will be listed next to the word "Sitemap," if you don't see it, we recommend you add it.

If you don't see your Sitemap in the Robots file, please note that it's common practice to have the primary Sitemap at the root of your domain link. For example:

https://www.example.com/**sitemap.xml**

It will pull up the full list of your website's URLs that are set to be found by search engines.

What is Schema Data?

Schema data (also known as structured data) for the business is a markup code that picks up on semantic vocabulary, enabling a better categorization of content for search bots to understand your content. Although Google scans and tries to understand all the information on your page, Googlebot likes to get validation of what it finds—this is where schema data comes in. It's designed specifically for Googlebot to get more information about your content.

Local SEO best practices include matching your primary Google Business Category as closely to your schema business category and also including at least the following:

- Business type
- Business name
- Description
- Local phone number (matching GBP)
- Address and location information
- Hours of operation
- Image URL
- Website URL
- Location and Map information
- List of other similar pages about your business
- Links to your social media profiles
- Areas you serve

It is recommended to also consider other structure data related to reviews and services that are important for home service businesses.

What Is On-Page SEO?

On-page SEO, also known as on-site SEO, refers to SEO techniques used to enhance the ability of your content to rank by making it more search-friendly. The primary goal of on-page SEO is to provide a better user experience and ensure that search engines can understand and rank the page appropriately.

But before you optimize, you need to start with a good topic and helpful content.

Keywords/topics: The content creation process needs to include research and analysis related to what users are interested in or searching for. For instance, this could be related to "your service" + "your city" or reviewing what people are asking about related to your services on Google or third-party websites and writing about that topic.

Content: High-quality content is one of the most important parts of on-page optimization. The following are practices that will help you get optimal results:

- Create high-quality, valuable, and relevant content that addresses the needs and interests of your target audience.
- Use proper grammar and spelling, and ensure content is well-structured and easy to read.

- Aim for longer-form content when appropriate, as it tends to perform better in search results by allowing the topic to be covered in more detail.

- Regularly update and refresh your content to keep it relevant and up-to-date as popular pages that are well-maintained can continue to attract organic traffic over time.

- Ensure that each page has unique content to avoid issues with keyword cannibalization (when two of your pages have the ability to rank for the search terms), or worse, duplicate content penalties.

Once we have our topic and content, we can start optimizing.

The following on-page SEO elements are essential:

Meta titles: A unique and descriptive title tag for each page, including your target keyword, topic, service and/or service area. Google will often display this information on the search results page. Keep title tags concise (around 60 characters) to ensure they display properly in search results.

Meta descriptions: Write compelling meta descriptions that summarize the page's content and encourage click-through rates. Descriptions should be around 150-160 characters and include relevant keywords, topics and information for users.

Header tags: Use title header tags to structure your content logically. The H1 tag should represent the main topic, followed by H2, H3, and so on for subtopics. Incorporate keywords in header tags when appropriate.

URL structure: Create clean and descriptive URLs that include keywords where relevant.

Image optimization and ALT tags: Compress and optimize images for faster loading times. Use descriptive file names and alt tags for images, including relevant keywords.

Internal linking: Link to other relevant pages within your website to improve navigation and provide context to search engines. Ensure that anchor text for internal links is descriptive and relevant.

Since content is fundamental to ranking in Google, let's explore content even further! Quality local content is where you create local service pages, local blogs, and geo pages that are keyword optimized.

What Kind of Local Content is Helpful for Home Service Businesses?

- **Service Pages**: Expanding on your services by using local SEO allows you to create quality content that is relevant. Service pages are meant to educate and convince a potential prospect to choose your services. With a local on-page SEO strategy, you will target residents in your area. This gives you an opportunity to be specific to their needs.

PRO TIP: Create a service page for every primary service you want to rank for.

- **Blogs**: Unlike service pages, local blogs are designed to provide free value to your reader. Provide local residents with tips and how-to guides that reflect the work you do and build trust. Check out Chapter 7 for in-depth information and topic ideas.

PRO TIP: Look for longer keyword phrases to discover opportunities to educate and inform homeowners who are related to your services.

- **Areas Served Pages (Geo Pages)**: Geo pages target surrounding areas that are within the proximity of your town or city. Local content of this kind boosts the growth of your brand within those areas. By including nearby cities and neighborhoods, you tell potential customers in other areas that your home service business is not restricted to just one city.

PRO TIP: Create a unique page with helpful content and resources for each area you serve.

Why Are Internal Links Important?

Internal links help improve your website's domain authority and help Google understand your content better. With internal linking, you make your site more user-friendly, which can increase your chances of higher rankings. And for technical SEO purposes, it's easier for Google to crawl and find your pages to index them.

What Is Off-Page SEO?

Off-page or off-site SEO refers to links from other websites. If you create valuable localized content like blogs, others may link to you, or you may reach out to nearby businesses with an effort to help them expand on a topic you are an expert in by linking to your page. It is the practice of improving your ranking outside your website through guest posting or social media marketing.

Conclusion

You might not have expected website optimization to involve so many little details. But the path to a successful website also requires a lot of patience and planning. Plus, user experience is a fundamental aspect of web design and integral to the overall success of SEO.

Let's summarize the essentials of this chapter:

- When choosing your website design, pick a website format that you consider user-friendly and most beneficial for your business.

- Content management systems are user-friendly, SEO-friendly, cost-effective, and best for regular content creation.

- Optimize your website for all types of screens, with a high priority on mobile devices.

- Keep in mind the colors and structure of your website, as it will determine user experience and shape the quality of your SEO.

- Localize your website so Google knows you are targeting customers in your area, and it will rank your content accordingly.

- Write high-quality content with the user in mind. Following on-page SEO best practices, including well-written and structured body copy, meta titles, descriptions, heading, image alt tags, and proper URL structures.

CHAPTER 6: HOW TO GET KEYWORD RESEARCH RIGHT FOR YOUR BUSINESS

In this chapter, you'll become familiar with:

- The importance of researching topics and themes
- Evaluation methods of keywords and key phrases
- Popular SEO analysis tools
- Components of on-page SEO

Optimizing your website to make it easy for prospective customers to find you is the most essential part of increasing visibility, and nobody knows your business better than you. But that is not the only crucial part of your keyword or content topic research. You must put yourself in your ideal customer's shoes and ask yourself the terms and phrases they use to describe your type of niche. They are probably not experts in that area, so it will take a bit of research for you to understand what they are looking for. From brainstorming lists of topics to finding relevant questions or terms and analyzing keyword data, lots of small steps and details must be considered.

Once you grasp proper research techniques, you are one step closer to offering value to your target audience. Every business owner's homework begins with an in-depth content topic and keyword research project that can be easily managed with the right tools and techniques.

How Research For SEO Works

Topic and keyword research for SEO is an important process that you need to complete before your on-page optimization. The first step is to understand your target audience's struggles and then set the goal of reaching out to them.

But the question is *how*?

Since the point of topic and keyword research is to identify what your target audience is searching for, you want to put yourself in their position. What terms do they use? Once you've identified key terms, you can find out how they're ranking in search engines. From technical to non-technical terms, this can be a time-consuming process. Along with research and planning, you need a supporting tool to go about your detailed market research.

Define Your Niche, Goals, and Target Audience

The steps that appear to be the most obvious and easiest are often the toughest part of the process. Defining your niche market and refining it takes time. When you list yourself as a "home service provider," you may not get many hits due to the hundreds of home service providers in your local area. However, if you narrow it down to "HVAC service" or "plumbing service," you'll be one step closer to meeting your future customer's needs.

Your ultimate goal with topic and keyword optimization is to increase organic traffic, as well as customer engagement, and drive sales. But even with the right research, success doesn't happen overnight. When making your local business visible to customers, you should take the appropriate steps, or in other words, set small goals that will eventually get you closer to the main goal.

At this early stage, you're still testing the waters, but it is an essential phase as it gives you an opportunity for future improvements. With your main goal in mind, you must measure your current performance regularly, ensuring that your small steps align with your main company goals.

Besides your niche and goals, defining your target audience is the third most important part of your research. In order to successfully define this specific group of consumers, you must know their demographics, geographic locations, and key interests. For example, local businesses in the home service industry may target homeowners in their mid-30s to late 60s with older homes that require interior and exterior repairs.

Luckily, there are useful keyword research tools that can help you gather all the information you need to effectively boost your SEO strategy. These tools will help you analyze behavioral data and even measure the effectiveness of your competition's marketing efforts.

Create a Relevant List of Topics and Break It Down

Having mentioned HVAC and plumbing services above, let's stick with the same example. To create a list of topics within this industry, you may want to expand on sub-categorical topics like "water heater installation" or "gas line repair." This will enable a more precise online search for users who are specifically interested in these services. Of course, you should focus on your business's strengths and prioritize your top services. If "water heater installation" is not your priority, you can expand on "gas line replacement" or "gas fitting services," for example. Make a relevant list of every service you provide and note down all the common key phrases and terms.

It's always worth checking out the keyword frequency (how often the keywords are searched) and also looking at seasonality (when they are being searched) between two comparable or even contrasting services. If one term appears to rank higher than the other, be sure to also analyze potential synonyms (e.g., "drain cleaning" versus "hydro jetting").

Which Search Terms Does Your Audience Use? How Do Those Keywords Rank Locally?

To expand on the point above, a keyword research tool will pull all the common industry keywords for you, along with how they rank in search engines.

One important aspect to keep in mind is localization. Since your goal is to target local customers, it is essential that you include your city in your main keyword phrase. Good examples would be "Dallas + gas line repair" or "gas line repair + Dallas TX." However, you might discover something else during your keyword research. Your potential customers might also be searching for "gas leak detection" or "gas line repair near me." It's essential that you list the terms and phrases your potential customers are using most often and check them for keyword difficulty, which is commonly a factor of how many other pages exist about the same topic and how popular they are.

When talking about keyword difficulty, we refer to the SEO metric that forewarns how difficult it might be to rank for that keyword. A high keyword difficulty indicates that your competition fights hard to rank high with that term. If you choose to compete for the same term, it will require a lot of effort on your part to keep up with them. If you happen to find low-competition keywords that are relevant to your services, you'll be able to rank without much effort. Often, localization to the city in the keyword makes a difference to the level of difficulty and can even reduce it.

How Are Your Competitors Ranking With Your Chosen Keywords? How Can You Do Better?

Tracking and analyzing how your competitors are ranking is a good way of teaching yourself how to do better. Create a list of top competitors that appear on the Search Engine Result Page (SERP) and apply a competitive analysis template to keep track of their actions. It's possible that you might identify content or keyword gaps that they missed, or the gaps are not relevant to them but to you. This will highlight a slight difference between your target audience and theirs. So it becomes essential that you create audience-focused content to fill those gaps.

With an SEO competitor analysis tool, you'll be able to track other businesses' performance on a regular basis. This will enable you to continuously work towards your SEO goals until you eventually outrank your local competition.

Where Do You Stand in Your Industry Locally, Nationally, and Globally?

As a local business, you must know exactly where you stand in your industry. By that, we mean your online presence and position in your local search engine ranking. There is no doubt that millions of consumers are in need of your services nationwide. But it is likely your objective to reach the local ones you and your team can service.

This is when localization plays an important role in your topic and keyword research. You want to make yourself available to your local community that is in proximity to your business location. You might have gathered all the essential keywords you need for your niche, but in order to achieve your goals and attract your target audience, you must localize those keywords so they filter out the national or global data. Unless you offer remote services or deliver products worldwide, there is no point for your business to be globally present. However, this doesn't mean that trying to rank well globally is a waste of time. By the time you've reached your main SEO goals, there are always opportunities to improve your website's authority with quality content that addresses global needs. For example, national blogs can be designed to address global household issues, for which you offer valuable information to a larger range of homeowners.

After all, you want to be more accessible to local clients and outperform other local competitors.

Popular Keyword Research Tools

While factoring in all of these components may seem daunting, there are free and subscription-based keyword research tools that will effectively help you through the process.

The leading SEO tools currently include:

- Ahrefs
- Moz
- SEMrush

Other helpful research tools and sites include:

- Answer the Public
- BuzzSumo
- SEO Powersuite
- Quora
- Google Trends
- Google Keyword Planner

- Website Auditor

How to Optimize Your Website With Keyword Research

Once you have completed your keyword research, including defining your niche, goals, and target audience, it's time to apply the results to your website's content. With your competitors' performance in mind, you want to make sure your website ranks in the organic listings with your chosen keywords.

If it is your first time building a website, make sure you choose a user-friendly template that is easy to navigate. Home service providers typically have at least these six menu sections: Home, About Us, Services, Why Hire Us, Testimonials, and Contact Us.

Ensure you start with great content and then optimize your pages for the main page, core services pages, subpages, and blogs, following the best practices examined in Chapter 5. Each page, especially core service pages, should be properly optimized from an SEO perspective. This way, Google's search engine will understand the relevance of those pages.

On-Page Optimization

On-page SEO optimization is not merely about creating content. It's also about how to strategically highlight your chosen keywords in:

- Title tags
- H1 tags (headers and subheaders)
- Images
- URLs
- Anchor texts
- XML sitemaps

Including your localized keywords in the above-mentioned items helps Google recognize your website's relevance. As a result, it will crawl all significant pages and start the ranking process. For an overview of on-page SEO practices, please review Chapter 5.

It's recommended to organize each page on your website and to create localized pages. Service pages especially have a strong potential to build up website authority.

Increase Your Website Authority

Increasing your website's authority, or domain authority, can be done when you are consistently providing value and becoming popular on Google.

Below is a list of what you can do to help influence your authority online:

Write high-quality content: Write content that your ideal customer values, based on topic and keyword research, and make it user-friendly, then ensure you follow on-page SEO practices to make it search-friendly. This means including your winning keywords in your H1 tags and meta titles and descriptions to help make it more search-friendly.

Optimize your content: You can optimize your content for relevant keywords by conducting keyword research and using them naturally in your content. Ensure your meta titles, descriptions, and headers are well-optimized for SEO.

Earn backlinks: Backlinks (also known as external links) are a form of link building where other websites point to your website. These can come naturally to you through good content but usually require some outreach to local or related websites. These signals help Google see you as more popular, which usually results in an increase in your rankings. It could be something as simple as reaching out to a local blogger and seeing if they would link to a resource you created on a page that can help their audience get additional and expert information that's complimentary to the topic of their blog. For example, a local blogger writes about their experience with a renovation, and you notice that they also talk about plumbing (but not in great detail). Asking them to link to one of your resource pages may be appropriate and beneficial to their local readers. This is effective because you have the potential to get real, local traffic from their blog to your website, and Google also sees this as them recommending you.

Have internal links: We have mentioned URLs above, but there is more to applying internal links. For example, linking from one service page to another helps Google to find and index your pages. In short, internal links are a key factor in ranking high in Google.

Ensure Indexation: Google processes information via texts, images, and videos. If it's satisfied with the information provided, it crawls the page. In other words, it's recorded in Google's search index. This is essential for ranking purposes.

Technical SEO: Address technical SEO issues such as broken links, duplicate content, and XML sitemap optimization.

Make it mobile-friendly: On-page optimization is important for mobile users, given that mobile usage has increased to over 50%, whether it's to look up or book a service. Refrain from using Flash and Java plugins to ensure a mobile-friendly experience.

Optimize UX: Further providing a mobile-friendly experience, you want to ensure the overall user experience is optimal. This may include readable fonts, neutral designs, and simple site navigation.

Improve load time: Faster-loading pages can improve user experience and SEO rankings. Use tools like Google PageSpeed Insights to identify and address speed issues.

Social signals: Engage on social media platforms to increase your online presence and encourage sharing of your content.

Conclusion

The process of figuring out how to write high-quality content through topic and keyword research doesn't have to be difficult. Knowing your niche, goals, and target audience is the most important factor in the whole process. Once you have that nailed down, your topic and keyword research should be a straightforward yet experimental process. Keep in mind there is always room for improvement. And since algorithms change all the time, you want to repeat the same keyword research process on a periodic basis. Before you get terrified of algorithm changes, see them as an opportunity to do better. You can use your competitor's performance analysis to your advantage!

Let's summarize the above so you know the order of how to start:

- Define your niche, goals and target audience and create a list of topics they might need help with.
- Narrow down the topics to the most essential phrases people type into Google and also consider the synonyms and different variations.
- Set goals to rank locally by including your main service area in the keyword phrase.
- Get an SEO tool that can create an SEO competitor analysis to help you keep up with the competition and even outrank them.

Once you have your topic and keyword research right, you'll be all set for your on-page optimization to drive organic traffic and build on your domain authority.

CHAPTER 7: LOCAL VS. HYPER-LOCAL CONTENT: MASTERING YOUR SERVICE AREA SEO GAME

In this chapter, you'll learn:

- What hyper-local vs. local really means
- Examples and practical uses
- How local and hyper-local strategies work together

Imagine you're a home service pro trying to stand out in the digital jungle. You've heard about local SEO, but did you know there's a secret weapon called hyper-local content? Let's dive into the world of geo-targeted content and see how it can skyrocket your online visibility.

Local Content: Casting a Wide (But Not Too Wide) Net

Local content is like throwing a party for your entire city. It's designed to get you noticed by homeowners in your general area. Here's what makes local content tick:

City-Slicker Keywords: Sprinkle your content with city or region-specific terms. It's like leaving a trail of digital breadcrumbs for potential customers. Example: "Best Plumbing Solutions in Atlanta"—simple, effective, and *local.*

Community Chatter: Talk about what's happening in your city. It shows you're not just a business, you're a neighbor. Example: "Beat the New York Heat: HVAC Tips for Sweaty City Dwellers."

Local SEO Wizardry: This is where you pull out the big guns—accurate business listings, local backlinks, and consistent NAP (Name, Address, Phone) info across the web. Example: Host a "Green Thumb Workshop" for Seattle gardeners, and watch those local links grow!

Did you know? A whopping 46% of all Google searches are looking for local information. That's nearly half of all searches!

Hyper-Local Content: Getting Up Close and Personal

Let's zoom in even further. Hyper-local content is like hosting a block party. It's intimate, specific, and tailored to homeowners right around the corner.

Neighborhood Knowhow: Create content that speaks directly to specific areas or even local streets. Example: "Battling Basement Bugs: A South Lake Union Homeowner's Guide"

Right Here, Right Now: Hyper-local content addresses immediate, relevant issues. Example: "Winter is Coming: North End's Old Home Heating Hacks"

Engagement on Steroids: By being ultra-specific, you're more likely to get people talking and sharing. Example: "This Week Only: 20% Off Cleaning Service for Oak Street Residents!"

Fun Fact: 72% of consumers who did a local search visited a store within five miles. Talk about bringing online searches to your doorstep!

Why This One-Two Punch Matters for Your SEO

Combining local and hyper-local strategies is like having your cake and eating it too. Here's why it's a game-changer:

Search Engine Superstar: You'll show up more often in searches, both broad and narrow. Example: Target "Houston plumbing repair" and "emergency plumbing fixes in Montrose" to cover all your bases.

Engagement Explosion: When content hits home, people can't help but interact. Example: A post about "5 Hidden Gems in Riverside Park" could go viral among local residents.

Trust Falls: Become the go-to expert in your area by consistently addressing local issues. Example: Sponsor the annual "Downtown Clean-up Day" and watch your community cred soar.

Here's a Jaw-Dropper: "Near me" or "close by" type searches grew by more than 900% over two years. That's a whole lot of people looking for businesses just like yours!

Conclusion

Think of local content as your city-wide billboard and hyper-local content as your neighborhood flyer. Both are crucial for a well-rounded SEO strategy that not only attracts eyeballs but turns those views into handshakes and, ultimately, happy customers.

Remember, in the world of home services, being found is half the battle. By mastering both local and hyper-local content, you're not just putting yourself on the map, you are becoming the map. So go ahead, get local, get hyper-local, and watch your business become the talk of the town (and the search engines)!

CHAPTER 8: THE LOCAL CONTENT CREATION PROCESS AND WHY IT MATTERS FOR YOUR SEO STRATEGY

You'll learn about content creation and why it matters to your home service business:

- The importance of knowing your target audience
- Search intent and search behavior
- What Google's EEAT guidelines are
- What Local vs. Hyper-local means
- Significance of fresh content and internal links

If you are already aware of the importance of content marketing, you'll be surprised to learn how many integral components go into the whole picture. From blogs and e-books to images, infographics, and videos, content creation is designed to help home service providers develop a brand and reach out to their target audience. Since you offer a wide range of local services, your marketing strategy must focus on targeting your local community.

This is where local content creation combined with local SEO helps your ideal customers narrow down their online search and find you. There is much to learn about the process and effectiveness of local content creation. There is also a right way of doing it to get the results you want. In this chapter, you will learn about the local content creation process and why it is important for your overall SEO strategy.

Why Local Content Creation is So Important

In regard to ranking in local search results and Maps, you may wonder what happened because, back in the day, it was easier to rank for results in your service area. Just using a combination of the top business citations with your NAP combined with local data on your site was all Google needed to put you on top of the SERP.

So what has changed?

Over time, just having the basics and being a part of local directory listings has become no longer sufficient, and as your competitors got smarter with SEO, it has gotten more difficult to maintain the top position. That's where engagement from content comes in.

Quality content plays a huge role in search engine rankings. Good copy increases your company's credibility as it can convince a reader to purchase a service or product. And by localizing your copy, you are increasing the chances of a sale because most people love to support local! It's a value-added convenience that you give to your potential customers.

Local content is important for home service businesses for several reasons:

- **Relevance to Local Customers**: Local content helps home service businesses connect with their local customers by creating content that is relevant to their specific needs, preferences, and concerns. This can help build trust and loyalty among customers, who are more likely to use a service provider that understands their local community.

- **Search Engine Optimization (SEO)**: Quality local content also helps home service providers improve their rankings—especially when following best practices and targeting keywords and phrases that are specific to their local area. This makes it easier for potential customers to find you online and ultimately increases organic visibility while driving more traffic and leads to your website.

- **Competitive Advantage**: In the highly competitive home service industry, local content can provide a competitive advantage by differentiating a business from its competitors. Local content allows home service businesses to showcase their local expertise and knowledge. Moreover, business owners can highlight the benefits they have brought to past clients in the area and position themselves as the go-to provider for similar customers in need of the same services.

- **Building Community Relationships**: Local content also helps home service businesses build relationships with other local businesses, organizations, and community groups. This can lead to valuable partnerships and collaborations, as well as increased brand awareness and exposure, and possibly even backlinks. Once you have built strong relationships with your clients, you are more likely to benefit from customer retention.

What Does "Local" Mean for SEO?

A local business is defined by the physical presence of an organization that is stationed at a specific location. This means that your SEO strategy must focus on visibility within Google's local search results. Any target keywords and phrases that contain your product or service must be searchable in your local area.

It's important to understand how Google's search algorithms work and what their ranking results mean. Google looks at factors that involve topic relevance, keyword usage, content relevance, website usability, source credibility, localization, and other signals.

You might wonder how Google determines local ranking. In short, local results are based on the following factors we have previously mentioned in Chapter 2. But let's expand on them a bit more:

- **Relevance**: In terms of relevance, Google puts a high emphasis on providing personalized results to searchers. Local-focused content doesn't only bring up services that are closest to you. In fact, the results most relevant to your needs will be listed at the top of the page. Optimized SEO in your business information helps Google match you with relevant searches. Relevance matters in terms of local citations (Google Business Profile), content, on-site SEO, and review recency.

- **Proximity**: Distance determines the proximity between the potential customer and your local business. Even when the online searcher doesn't indicate a location, Google will base its search on the user's data collection and calculate the distance accordingly. This is when local businesses will pop up on the search results page because they provide local significance that may be relevant to the user. That said, a business may also have global significance if Google believes its content is of interest to people outside the radius of the target area. But as a local business, it is highly important to focus on local content creation combined with local SEO best practices. With the right strategy, you can rely on Google to push you to the top of the local search result page.

- **Prominence**: The local prominence score is based on your business's popularity online and combines both relevance and distance. Your level of popularity is determined by high-quality reviews, news articles, and blogs about you written by credible sources. Since prominence refers to the visibility and authority of your business and website in its specific geographic area, it is crucial to follow all the GBP and SEO best practices. Also, acquiring links to articles from other local businesses, postings, and social media signals gives your home service business additional credibility and trustworthiness, as these individuals have either actively experienced or are aware of your business or services within your service area.

4 Common Types of Search Intent

People conduct an online search with a goal in mind. If you are hoping to help them meet that goal, it's important to understand the four different categories of a user's search intent. Otherwise, you might not target the right people and end up missing the opportunity to provide the value you intended for your specific audience. Therefore, it's best to factor in these components to help them find what they are looking for when working on your local SEO strategy. That's where the concept of keyword intent comes in.

Keyword intent is all about understanding why someone uses a particular word or phrase in their search. Once you have zeroed in on this important piece of information, understanding what the user will do with the results they find is paramount.

Here are the four most common types of search intent to be aware of:

Informational

This is where users seek information or answers to specific questions. These results are primarily designed to educate but can also be effective for online educators who want to create funnel traffic to gain subscribers. Providing informational content is ideal for home service providers to drive conversions, and this can be achieved through local blog posts.

A blog post about "How to Prevent Frozen Pipes in Winter" is a good example. Mr. Rooter Plumbing franchisees, especially in Canada, can create a blog post or video explaining the steps homeowners can take to prevent their pipes from freezing during winter. This content establishes the company as a trusted source of plumbing advice.

Commercial

Indicates that the user is in the research and consideration phase, seeking information to make a future purchase decision. Here is where a searcher seeks to learn more about different brands, whether they are services, retail items, or other products. The goal is to gather enough information to help them make an informed decision about a potential job booking or purchase that will suit their needs. For home service businesses, it is crucial to stand out in terms of relevance, distance, and prominence. Searchers will most likely compare reviews, want to better understand your experience, and ensure you're within their geographical region.

For example, with "Mr. Rooter Mississauga Reviews," Mr. Rooter Plumbing of Mississauga ON can optimize its page and Google Profile to highlight the benefits of its plumbing services, such as certified technicians, years of experience, workmanship guarantees, and customer reviews.

Transactional

Transactional search intents are related to the goal of making a purchase. This search type implies that the user is ready to make a purchase or take action right away. In addition to appearing in organic search results, a common strategy is to also run paid ads targeting transactional intent searches. When targeting transactional search intents, your motivation is based on immediate sales. So it is crucial to have a clear, unique selling proposition on the landing page. It should also offer compelling benefits and a strong call to action.

A search for "emergency plumbing service in Vancouver" is an example of transactional search intent. A dedicated landing page that highlights Mr. Rooter Plumbing's 24/7 emergency plumbing service includes a phone number for immediate contact and emphasizes the urgency of the situation.

Navigational

When looking for a specific website, users type keywords into Google that will pull up the relevant website or business's physical location. The best way to simplify a search for searchers is by optimizing your company's branded keywords and fixing any SEO issues you may have. You don't want your potential customer to accidentally be navigated to a competitor. When using high-quality content on a consistent basis, you won't experience this risk as you'll continue to rank well organically.

For example, consider a search for "Mr. Rooter Plumbing website." The homepage of Mr. Rooter Plumbing should be optimized to appear prominently in search results when users search for the company's name. It should also provide easy navigation to different plumbing services and locations served.

EEAT Guidelines

Google Search Quality Evaluation guidelines include EEAT guidelines, but many commonly refer to these as Google's EEAT guidelines. EEAT refers to the "experience, expertise, authoritativeness, and trustworthiness" of the content published on websites. These guidelines are part of Google's efforts to ensure that its search results display high-quality content that is useful and reliable for users.

EEAT guidelines provide recommendations for content creators and website owners to improve:

- Quality of content by demonstrating expertise
- Establish trustworthiness through accurate and well-researched information
- User experience by keeping the website navigation simple and flawless

Here are some key points of the EEAT guidelines:

1. **Expertise**: Content creators should demonstrate expertise in their field by providing accurate, high-quality, and comprehensive information. This can be achieved through author biographies, credentials and by citing reputable sources.

2. **Authoritativeness**: Content should be written by authors who are recognized as authorities in their field. Websites should also have a strong reputation and be well-respected within their industry.

3. **Trustworthiness**: Trustworthiness can be established through accurate and well-researched information, transparency about sources and affiliations, and avoiding misleading or deceptive practices.

4. **User experience**: Websites should be easy to navigate and provide a good user experience. This includes having a clear layout, good design, and fast page load times.

In short, EEAT guidelines are important because they help to ensure that users can trust the information they find in search results. By promoting high-quality content that is both useful and reliable, Google can provide a better experience for users and maintain its position as the leading search engine. Adhering to these guidelines can also help website owners improve their search engine rankings and gain more traffic to their sites.

What Makes Content High-Quality?

Once you understand the EEAT guidelines, you can apply that knowledge to your content structure. Ensuring that your content has nested headers and subheaders, such as H1, H2, and H3, is important in terms of helping the reader navigate and understand the content. Plus, consistency plays a huge role in content quality, which is why you want to adopt the habit of posting regularly and keeping it fresh. In order to do so, periodic updates are recommended; content might need to be re-optimized after new keyword research. There might be new trends or changing Google algorithms that come with new opportunities for you to update your content. Or perhaps your industry has introduced innovative technology that you want to inform readers about.

Creating helpful, engaging, and concise long-form content that is optimized to rank well in SERPs will also increase the time spent by searchers on your site and lower the bounce rate.

Google Loves Fresh Content!

This brings us closer to why content marketing strategies are crucial for maintaining relevance. Adding ongoing relevant content and updates to your website is what your audience and Google want to see!

The problem with Google's ever-changing algorithm is that any existing piece of content can become stagnant or outdated. Just because you have a great website with the right title tags and all the best links does not mean you will not get discounted if Google doesn't see fresh information posted on a consistent basis, and this makes sense. Online searchers seek relevancy and will always opt for the most recent piece of content as it provides the assurance that the writer is aware of recent changes.

To keep your content up-to-date, you need a methodology where you create and post content to your website on a regular basis. Luckily, there is a framework for figuring out what kind of content to write, why it should be written, and how to do it consistently.

First, you should understand and accept that you must become a subject-matter expert. Even when you are not a writer or a content creator, being a subject-matter expert means there are things you know that the general population does not. Your valuable knowledge and expertise in the service you offer are why local residents hire you. Plus, you have a qualified team of people who are also proficient in this field. This gives you the power to create content on the topic that you know most about.

Your field of work will likely contain a variety of different topics, including one to two relevant keywords. You may not think it at first, but there is a wide range of different topics in your industry that will make strong pieces of content.

Types of Content

Content doesn't have to be restricted to just written words in an article or blog post. Content comes in a variety of forms, with the most popular being articles, photos, videos, and audio files. Stop and think about what content creation method might work best for you.

A talented writer focuses on writing quality blogs and articles, whereas a person proficient with cameras produces photos and videos. Articulate and outspoken people like to talk, so they have podcasts. Content creation can be done in many different, creative ways, all of which are suitable for your home service business in one way or another.

Whether it is a blog, YouTube video, or Vimeo link, one piece of content can create multiple valuable links that navigate toward your website. Transcribing words from a video can also generate valuable content.

Content Consistency

Besides creating content consistently, linking and syndicating it to other platforms helps you keep it fresh. At the same time, these link building opportunities will boost your domain authority and help your website rank at the top of the SERP. This type of local content creation can maximize your rank potential in your area. Depending on your industry, it might be highly competitive. Your competition might be trying to rank for the same keywords (unless they have invested in Google Ads for additional success in sales and conversion). But this is not the time to give up!

You made an effort to build a website and took your time to optimize it accordingly. Furthermore, you have link building and content development strategies in progress. Now is the time to start looking at organic content as well as Google Maps Optimization and getting ranked so your audience can find you.

How the Local Content Creation Process Works

Now that you understand the significance of content and SEO, we'll examine the steps of local content creation in greater detail. The road to successful local ranking, as mentioned above, is marked by relevance, distance, and prominence. With these three key factors in mind, you will be able to create a successful content marketing strategy for your home service business.

Local Keyword Research

During local topic and keyword research, an SEO expert conducts a search and analysis of search queries that users type into Google. The goal is to measure the volume of high-ranking keywords and determine which ones will work best for your website so they will target users in that specific area. The research process also involves identifying the keywords your competitors are ranking for.

Optimize Location Page

Your main location page (especially if you are a multi-location business or part of a franchise) serves as an introduction page that welcomes new local visitors. Location-specific websites should be inviting, transparent, and informative, providing enough value that will convert them into customers. When optimizing a location page, there are a few things to keep in mind:

- Focus on the main location only and ensure the NAP data is up-to-date
- Display your local phone number prominently on the page
- Include a map and directions
- Include relevant images and videos that are geotagged
- Provide links to products and services offered with clear descriptions containing optimized keywords and title tags
- Utilize a powerful call to action

When improving your local SEO, location pages can be a strong tool as long as they're done properly and follow the key factors of relevance, distance, and prominence.

Create Local Service Pages

When creating location-specific content, you want it to be unique and focused. Unlike blogs, the focal point of service pages is to identify and highlight your customers' pain points and offer a solution. Your goal is to attract more qualified visitors to your service page, so creating a local service can include:

Compelling Headline: Craft a clear and compelling headline that includes your primary keyword. It should immediately convey what the page is about and pique the visitor's interest.

Engaging Introduction: Write an engaging introduction that provides a brief overview of the service, its benefits, and its relevance to the visitor's needs or pain points.

Detailed Service Description: Provide a detailed description of the service, highlighting its features, advantages, and unique selling points (USPs). Use bullet points, subheadings, and visuals (such as images and videos) to make the content more scannable. Describe what your customers can expect when they hire your service. What is your procedure? What will you deliver?

Benefits and Value Proposition: Explain why prospects should choose you. Include a section explaining why your customers choose your service. What makes you stand out from the competition?

Client Testimonials and Reviews: Include testimonials from satisfied clients and, if applicable, case studies that showcase successful outcomes.

Social proof can greatly increase trust and conversions.

FAQ: You can be several steps ahead by including frequently asked questions from your customers. This is an added value that helps them better understand your services and what they will get out of them. It also shows that you, as the business owner, listen to your customers and care about meeting their needs.

Clear CTA: Use clear calls to action throughout the page. Remember to remind the reader of their pain points and why they need the solutions that only you can provide.

Schema Markup: Implement schema markup to provide search engines with structured data about your service, which can enhance your visibility in rich snippets.

SEO best practices: Carefully incorporate the keywords into your content, ensuring they are relevant and flow well with the overall text and are mentioned in the H1, H2, H3, etc. Also, include internal links to already established service pages that are relevant.

Create Areas Served/Geo Pages

Whether your business operates in a small town or a metropolis, there are various districts that are worth mentioning to boost your brand. Including an "areas we serve" page or section ensures that you are not restricted to just one place but are willing to travel within the city that you serve.

Geo pages are important for local rankings as they meet the key factors of relevance, distance, and prominence. They allow your home service business to branch out and reach out to potential customers within the proximity of your business location.

A geo page that targets a specific area in your city may typically include an introduction of services, as well as images and descriptions of recent work completed in the area. Depending on the relevancy of the service in a target community, you can coin the keyword with the location. That geo page may also include reviews from happy customers and other content, such as videos and infographics, to add more value. Linking to a team page is a great way to show appreciation to your staff, especially those who got a special mention from a customer in the reviews!

PRO TIP: Increase engagement by going hyper-local and narrowing down your focus to very specific areas, such as communities and neighborhoods in the areas you serve, and by addressing immediate concerns or interests of the local population.

Local Blogs

Local blogs allow for long-tail keywords (a search phrase made up of three or more words) and related search queries. Blogs can be particularly important for link building because websites and publishers don't typically like linking to home pages, location pages, or service pages.

Local blogs can include a wide range of topics but can also be designed to help readers solve problems. They include maintenance information, valuable tips and how-to's, but also allow you to tie in advice from your company's perspective and introduce a product or service. A local blog is also an ideal tool for establishing social media posts and reaching out to other potential customers. From brand awareness to increasing visibility and organic traffic, blogging is one of the key elements of your local marketing strategy. Blogs also build trust with potential customers because they don't feel like they are being sold something or convinced to purchase a service. Rather, they are given valuable information free of charge, which is seen as courteous and trustworthy. More on this and the content marketing journey searchers take in Chapter 9.

Resource Pages

A resource page or reference page is a section on your website that provides your readers with useful recommendations or additional information about your industry. It could include links to validated resources or even a partner company's website that you advocate for. Resource guides, educational pages, case studies, or online courses are also highly effective.

Tips On What to Do When Writing

Proofreading

It takes time to create helpful high-quality content. Many others have tackled similar, if not the exact same, topics you are now. As you can imagine, it's incredibly important to stand out. Even when adopting your own unique voice, there will always be some similarities to other published content. It helps to run the text through a plagiarism tool like Grammarly to ensure your content is unique and original.

When writing content, while your focus is on creating a high-value piece, typos and grammar can be found and corrected in the draft stage. Having an experienced proofreader go through the text can help address these errors, as well as structural issues, clarity, and misplaced commas.

Beware of Keyword Stuffing and Keyword Cannibalization

Besides proofreading, it is important to review your content for keyword stuffing and keyword cannibalization. The former refers to an excessive use of a keyword that could lower your content quality. On the other hand, the latter is when multiple pages on your website are targeting, and therefore ranking, for the same keyword. This confuses Google in terms of which page they should prioritize.

Google can tell if your content provides value. If it does, it will greatly outweigh other criteria, such as keyword stuffing. However, that's not always the case. If you prefer to take your content analysis to a deeper level, consider using SEO keyword tools to measure the percentage and the uniqueness of the content.

PRO TIP: Keyword stuffing offers little to no improvement on the generative engine's response.

Insert Images and Video Content

Images and videos are useful visuals to enhance your local content. It's common for most visitors to skim a text and skip to the part they are looking for. But visuals, such as vlogs or infographics with listicles, are more likely to catch the reader's eye and have them stop scrolling. They will take a few moments to absorb the visual content. It helps decrease bounce rates, increases their time on the website, and still delivers value.

Fact Check

During a fact check, you will check for factual accuracy by thoroughly analyzing the source material and ensuring the information you're putting out there is reliable.

Having the subject matter expert involved in the process results in more accurate information, especially when they are involved at the beginning of the content planning. This results in more accurate information and better quality content.

Add Metadata and Schema Data

The metadata includes a title and description that helps Google's search engine understand your content. Whenever your page appears in a search, the title tag and description are what the user sees first. While they're optimized with local keywords, the title and description should also be compelling enough to increase the click-through rate.

Schema data, or metadata, should include additional information about your business type, location, hours, and contact info coded for search engines like Google to understand. Additional schema about your service, areas served, and review ratings can also help Google better understand your business.

Add Internal Links

During local content creation, perform internal linking to related pages and information if it's helpful to the reader. Link service pages to other pages and local blogs to other relevant local blogs. Not only does this show your reader that you have more to offer, but it also shows information hierarchy and can help increase your ranking power.

Refresh Old Content

Content refreshes, including updating and re-optimizing your pages to make them more up-to-date and relevant, are known to enhance your rankings. A refreshed piece of content tells the reader that you are relevant and have accurate information on your page. When online searchers see a recent date in the title tag, they're more likely to choose your source of information. Refreshed content also ensures Google that your page is still relevant and not outdated or stale. This also helps increase its metrics and overall performance in local and organic search results.

However, refreshing is not to be confused with repurposing. When repurposing a piece of content, the intent is to alter its original format by recycling relevant information and using it somewhere else.

Conclusion

Local content creation is designed to connect your home service business with your local community and the surrounding area. As you are situated in a particular town or city, it only makes sense that you target residents in close proximity to your office. The good news is that Google is well aware of that. Google gathers geographical data from users' browsers, settings, or applications when they conduct online searches. As long as you provide local content, you can use Google to direct these searches your way.

To finish off this chapter strong, let's summarize the key points:

- Local content creation targets residents in your area and gives you the opportunity to form a deep relationship with your community.

- Know local searchers' search intent and steer your content toward the intent you want to target.

- Be aware of the difference between service pages, geo pages, and local blog posts as they all serve different purposes.

- Follow the EETA guidelines to ensure you publish quality content that is easy to navigate and establishes trustworthiness in your local community.

- Proofread and analyze your content using an SEO keyword checker and plagiarism checker.

- Embellish your content with visuals and re-optimize and refresh old content to show online searchers you're aware of new trends.

- Provide helpful and informative content that homeowners would find beneficial and share with others.

CHAPTER 9: THE CUSTOMER JOURNEY

UNLOCKING THE POTENTIAL OF EFFECTIVE CONTENT MARKETING

In today's digital age, businesses are vying for the attention of their target audience in a highly competitive online landscape. Understanding content marketing and how to leverage it for engagement and conversions is crucial for all home service businesses. Throughout this chapter, we will provide a comprehensive explanation of the content marketing journey, using specific search queries as practical examples to illustrate how this works.

Effective content marketing will not only attract prospects but also move them through a content marketing funnel to drive more sales and grow your business. By having content built out at every stage, you have the ability to build trust by establishing your business as the expert. Effective content marketing efforts will also help the prospective customer discover your brand and strengthen brand awareness along their journey.

The customer content journey is best illustrated using an example, and we'll demonstrate this using the related search examples for "water heaters" below.

Step 1: Awareness – "Water heater dripping"

The content marketing journey begins with creating awareness about a particular problem or need that potential customers might have. In this example, the search query "water heater dripping" typed into Google represents a common issue faced by homeowners. Using voice search, the potential client might say, "Hey Google, tell me why my water heater is dripping" or "Hey Google, what are the most common reasons a water heater drips."

As a local business, you should create informative content that educates readers about the problem, its causes, and the potential consequences of ignoring it.

This could include blog posts, articles, or even videos explaining how to identify and temporarily fix the issue. By offering valuable information, you position yourself as an authority in the field, building trust with your audience.

PRO TIP: Improve results in the awareness stage by understanding the user's search intent and how they search. If the user is in an information-gathering stage and using Voice Search, ensure that frequently asked questions are covered to improve your chances of appearing in Google's AI overview.

Step 2: Consideration – "Water heater repair vs. replacement"

Once your target audience is aware of the problem, they start to consider different solutions. In the case of a leaking water heater, people might ponder whether it is more cost-effective to repair or replace the unit.

To cater to this stage, create content that provides objective comparisons, pros and cons, and expert opinions on both options. This could be in the form of a detailed blog post or a downloadable guide outlining the various factors to consider when making a decision. By giving your audience valuable insights and impartial advice, you establish credibility and position your brand as an industry leader.

PRO TIP: Using data, stats, or having a comparison table can significantly increase your chances of showing up in Google's AI overview.

Step 3: Decision Making/Conversion – "New water heater installation Dallas"

In this stage, potential customers have gathered information and are now ready to make a purchase decision. For those looking to install a new water heater in Dallas, they might search for specific terms like "new water heater installation Dallas." To capture their interest and drive conversions, your content should focus on showcasing your expertise and the benefits of choosing your services.

This can include photos of completed installs, case studies, customer testimonials, or even a comprehensive guide on the different types of water heaters available and the installation process. By demonstrating your professionalism and highlighting your unique selling points, you persuade potential customers to choose you over your competitors.

Step 4: Retention – "Water heater maintenance tips"

The journey doesn't end with a purchase; it continues with nurturing and retaining customers. After installing a new water heater, homeowners will be interested in learning how to maintain it for optimal performance—and they should know that this is something you can do for them. This is where your content can provide valuable after-sales support as well as future opportunities.

By sharing maintenance tips, best practices, and even troubleshooting guides, you build a relationship with your existing customers, positioning yourself as a trusted resource. Additionally, you increase the chances of customer loyalty and future referrals.

Conclusion

Understanding the content marketing journey is a pivotal part of successfully engaging your target audience and guiding them toward conversion. By aligning your content strategies with each stage—from awareness to conversion and retention—you can create a cohesive and effective content marketing campaign.

Remember, providing valuable and informative content at each step will help establish your brand as an authority, foster trust, and ultimately drive business growth. So, unlock the potential of content marketing and watch your digital presence flourish.

CHAPTER 10: ACQUIRING LOCAL LINKS IS CRITICAL FOR SEO—HERE'S HOW LINK BUILDING WORKS

Whitehat link building plays a huge role in the process of search engine optimization. As the term suggests, it involves networking with other marketers or business owners by collecting inbound links to your website. To improve your website's authority, it's crucial that you make use of referral traffic to increase visibility so your local clients are able to find you easily.

With local backlink building, always prioritize quality over quantity. Ensure that the websites linking to your business are reputable, relevant to your industry or service area, and have real traffic. When done right, you can benefit from real traffic from local websites that can discover your business and also get rewarded by Google's algorithm for having this valuable search signal.

Let's take a look at how effective link building is.

What is Link Building?

An important part of utilizing external links is ensuring that you collect useful links from local websites. This means that the page you are getting a link referral from should be complementary to the content on their website. This helps align the audience to be local homeowners who might be in need of your services at some time.

But what exactly is link building, and how do you successfully incorporate it into your SEO strategy?

Link building is like relationship building with other websites, webmasters, bloggers, and influencers. When the outreach is done the right way, you are creating mutually beneficial relationships or partnerships with others for your audience with content. When approached from a relationship and value-add perspective, link building can greatly enhance your authenticity and credibility in the eyes of Google. Therefore, successful links acquired this way can result in higher rankings on Google's search engine results page.

Link building involves various tactics and strategies to build high-quality links, both internally and externally.

Internal Links Vs. External Links

When speaking of internal links, we refer to a hyperlink that is located in the same domain (website). Internal links are basically links that connect different pages within the same website. This includes, for instance, linking to a service page from your blog or a link to a contact form. Internal links can help increase the average time spent on your website, which means the reader has found value.

That said, inbound links should be crawlable (follow) in order to be effective for SEO. Including a follow link will also increase your domain authority, telling site crawlers that your website is legitimate and relevant.

On the other hand, external links direct you to a different domain. An external link, also known as an outbound link or an outgoing link, is a hyperlink or URL that points from one webpage to a webpage that is hosted on a different domain. In other words, external links are links from other websites that point to your website. For instance, when you click on an external link on a webpage, it takes you to a different website or web address, often in a new browser tab or window.

This becomes particularly beneficial when another website has an external link that generates traffic to your website. In this case, the external links from the other website are a backlink to your website. External links act as endorsements and can significantly impact your website's visibility and rankings.

These link signals are an essential aspect of SEO and online visibility. Google sees these links as "referrals" from other websites, and the more referrals you have, the more popular your page can become in Google.

For example, a local home improvement and DIY website links to you for additional resources about your home service business. Having your services, resources or guides, in this case, creates valuable local backlinks that can connect homeowners throughout your city with you—a trusted local home service provider.

External links are also commonly used to connect web content and provide references, citations, or additional resources to the reader.

What is a Follow Link?

A "follow" link, also known as a "dofollow" link, is a hyperlink that search engines, like Google, consider when evaluating search ranking because they allow search engine crawlers to follow them and pass on their ranking value to the linked website. Follow links pass link equity or "link juice" from the linking page to the linked page, helping the linked page gain popularity and authority signals in search engine rankings.

To make a link follow, no additional attributes are needed. By default, all standard HTML links are "follow" links. The link type only changes when additional attributes are added to the HTML code. Example: <a href="https://www.example.com">Go to Example</a>

What is Link Equity?

Link equity is an SEO concept that refers to the value or authority signal that is passed from one web page to another through hyperlinks or backlinks when the links are "followed" by website crawlers.

Link equity is passed through follow links, but not no-follow links.

What is a No-Follow Link?

Contrarily, no-follow links instruct search engine crawlers not to follow or pass on any ranking value to the linked website.

A no-follow link is usually tagged to have a "nofollow" attribute, which informs search engines to ignore the SEO value of the link. The link signal will still be there, but the "nofollow" attribute instructs the crawler not to pass any link equity to the page. In addition to using HTML attributes, you can also use the meta robots tag to apply “nofollow” to all links on a specific page. Example: <a href=“https://example.com/” rel=“nofollow”>

Even though these links don’t pass link equity, no-follow links are still valuable because they provide brand recognition and referral traffic from potential customers.

No-follow links are commonly used for various reasons, including to prevent spam, control the flow of link equity, or indicate that a link is paid sponsorship or user-generated content.

What is a Sponsored Link?

A sponsored link attribute is used to indicate that a hyperlink is a result of a paid sponsorship, endorsement, or advertising arrangement. It is a way to inform search engines that the link should not be considered when calculating search engine ranking factors or passing link equity. In essence, it helps distinguish between organic links and paid or sponsored links.

Keep in mind that sponsoring a link is often not a long-term solution if you seek to rank high organically in your local area. If you want to build brand awareness and increase visibility, acquiring local links through link building is your best bet for long-term success.

What is a UGC (User-Generated Content) Link?

User-generated content (UGC) links are links tagged as user-generated content links so crawlers can better understand their origination. These links are commonly created by users on platforms like forums or comment sections. A UGC link for a home service business could come from a customer's review or testimonial posted on a review website, social media platform, or another website.

Although UCG links don't pass link equity, they can still be valuable for a home service business as they provide social proof, brand awareness and credibility to potential customers and can indirectly contribute to SEO and online visibility.

How Does Acquiring Local Links Impact an SEO Strategy?

Having covered the significance of link building above, acquiring "local links" has a huge impact on your overall SEO strategy. When an SEO expert improves your search engine ranking in your local area, they will acquire relevant backlinks from local businesses. This is to enable organic local search, as well as increase your visibility as a part of the SEO strategy.

Local links can help position your website accordingly in order to target local customers who are in need of your services or products. These are customers who live in close proximity to your business, and are in need of your services in the future or are ready to buy now. A local SEO strategy itself gives your potential customers a sense of your business's presence in search engines. If you know exactly what your target customers are searching for on the web, you can use that to your advantage with a well-organized and executed local links campaign. Whether it is a backlink from a renowned local business or a related type of site, a local link specifically targets potential buyers in your area. While this greatly strengthens your SEO strategy in the form of increased domain authority, it also delivers more enhanced search traffic.

Your ultimate goal is to drive ongoing organic traffic to your website. That's when local links—both internal and external—help your website's content rank high. They ensure your website's content is relevant to what people search for in your service area. Securing organic traffic with local links is essential for your SEO practice and has a positive long-term impact on your overall marketing strategy.

The Link Building Process

Building links can be a challenging task that requires thorough planning and the implementation of effective strategies. Plus, you must examine other local businesses and how they have set up their website and Google Business Profiles. Focus on quality over quantity because not all local business owners have high domain authority, so they could do you more harm than good.

Each sub-section below will explain what they are, plus their role and importance in link building.

SEO Planning

Before embarking on any link building campaign, proper planning is essential. SEO planning involves setting objectives, identifying target audiences, and determining the local link building strategies that will yield the best results.

Your SEO planning process begins with knowing where your target audience is online, what questions they are seeking answers to, and what keywords they are searching. You need to perform topic and keyword research. This step includes performing a deep dive into identifying target topics and keywords, performing competitor analysis, and understanding the local link building landscape.

When you plan a local link building strategy, you should have your local community in mind. Link building is about relationship building, so it's important to lead with quality and be genuinely helpful, usually by sharing, updating, or creating new content.

The research and planning stage will also help determine the type of content and key strategy that should be used for link acquisition, which is covered in the next section.

But, before determining what content will be used or establishing a consistent content creation or blogging routine, it is essential to thoroughly analyze questions and search terms to help identify specific long-tail keywords within your target location. Next, evaluate the websites related to your business category or talk about your services and identify opportunities your content can potentially be added to add value. In the planning step, double-check the external websites by measuring web page metrics, including traffic, quality and spam score. Here, we recommend steering clear of spammy websites that don't have any real traffic.

When the planning stage is done, you will have a roadmap of what local websites are a good candidate to link to and what type of content you need to use.

The next crucial part of your SEO planning includes determining who to contact and the best way to do so to get a reply.

Prospecting

Prospecting is the process of identifying and finding potential link opportunities or sources for building backlinks to a website. It includes identifying and discovering potential websites, blogs, or online platforms that could be valuable sources for acquiring backlinks to your own website. This step is crucial in building a list of opportunities for outreach and collaboration.

By using various prospecting techniques, such as advanced search queries and competitor research, you can compile a list of potential link sources. Effective prospecting involves finding websites that are relevant to your niche or industry and have the potential to provide high-quality, authoritative, and relevant backlinks.

When this step is done, you will have a list of prospects for link sources and a communication strategy for outreach.

Outreach

The process of outreach involves reaching out to potential partners like website owners, influencers or collaborators to pitch an idea or piece of content that is relevant and helpful to them or their audience.

Outreach involves researching, personalizing and reaching out to these sources and establishing a connection. Personalized and well-crafted communication is crucial in engaging potential link partners through personalized outreach to acquire links from relevant and authoritative sources. This is effective through email, social messages, or even contact forms and phone.

People are busy, so it might be a time-consuming process that involves various follow-ups via email or social media. When approaching new potential partners, be sure to use personalized information and be genuine so they know you did your research about them. Be precise and transparent about your motivations and highlight how your goals will benefit them.

Building relationships and engaging in meaningful conversations are vital to obtaining high-quality local links. To do this successfully, personalized multi-channel follow-ups work best.

Link Placement

Link placement is the final step in the local link building process. Once you have successfully engaged with potential link partners, it is time to secure the link placement. This can be achieved through guest blog posts, resource page suggestions, partnerships, or press releases.

Other important yet tricky parts of local link building are negotiating content topics, adding new content, and making updates. Clear communication and attention to detail are extremely important. Also, negotiate with your collaborator about further placements or updates to continue building good relationships with their website and highlight how it will benefit them.

When securing a link placement, ensure that the link is contextually relevant, naturally integrated, and placed on a highly authoritative and relevant page. Aim for in-content links with appropriate anchor text, which is the clickable text used in a hyperlink. Optimize it for relevant keywords to increase the SEO value of the backlink. The quality and relevance of the linking page and domain are critical factors that search engines consider when evaluating the value of a link.

Once you secure the backlinks, it's also important that you continue monitoring its performance. Ensure they remain active and that the linking page maintains its authority over time. If any issues arise, follow up and work on resolving them to maintain the link's effectiveness.

By understanding and effectively implementing these four components—SEO planning, prospecting, outreach, and link placement—in your local link building process, you can increase your website's visibility, attract a local audience, and improve your search engine rankings. Remember that building high-quality links takes time and effort, but the results are well worth it. Plan your strategy carefully, prospect wisely, engage thoughtfully, and secure valuable link placements to enhance your local online presence.

Key Link Building Strategies

Each section below will explain important link building strategies, plus their role and importance in link building.

Help a Reporter Out (HARO)

HARO link building is all about responding to journalists' queries to gain media mentions and high-quality backlinks. HARO is an expert's source that connects reporters, content writers, and freelancers. When utilizing the right techniques (such as setting the right email filters), HARO can have a positive impact on your link building efforts and even increase your brand awareness. Participating in HARO link building allows your business to provide expert opinions and gain exposure in relevant publications while securing authoritative backlinks.

That said, it can be a very time-consuming process that involves sifting through a high number of emails daily and staying in regular contact with journalists. Respond promptly and provide insightful, concise, and newsworthy contributions to increase your chances of being featured. Ensure your responses align with the journalist's requirements and publication guidelines.

Expert insights, quotes, data, or case studies that can add value to news articles or blog posts in your industry.

Community Involvement and Sponsorships

Supporting local events, charities, or causes through sponsorships and active participation is an effective way to garner mentions and links. By aligning your business with local events, sports teams, or charitable initiatives, you can receive online recognition and links from event organizers or participants. The key is to choose sponsorships that align with your business values and resonate with your target audience. Content for this strategy includes event promotions, sponsor recognition on websites or event materials, and updates on social media platforms.

Local News and PR Coverage

Generating local news coverage or crafting compelling press releases about your business can significantly impact your local link building efforts. The goal here is to create newsworthy stories related to your business, events, or achievements and pitch them to local media outlets. Securing media coverage can result in natural backlinks from news articles, boosting your online visibility and credibility. When crafting your story, emphasize its uniqueness and the positive impact it has on your local community. Content types for this strategy include press releases, news articles, and mentions in the media.

Guest Blogging

Guest blogging is a powerful strategy that involves collaborating with other websites in your industry to create valuable, informative content, usually with a link back to one of your pages in it. Guest blogging, or guest posting, is an effective way to secure backlinks from authoritative websites. Offer high-quality, unique content to relevant websites in your industry. Guest posting not only helps with link building but also positions you as an industry expert. This approach helps you position yourself as an industry expert while earning backlinks from reputable sources within your niche. To make the most of guest blogging, it's crucial to identify websites that have a strong local presence and a relevant audience. Additionally, ensure that your guest posts focus on providing genuine value rather than being overly promotional. High-quality articles, blog posts, or how-to guides are commonly used as content for this strategy.

Resource Page Building

Developing comprehensive resource pages specific to your local area to attract links from local websites is another strategy that you can use to acquire links. The primary goal is to provide valuable information to your target audience while positioning your website as an authoritative source of local knowledge.

Resource page link building involves acquiring backlinks from relevant resource pages on other websites, which curate and list helpful links, tools, and information related to a specific niche or industry.

Resource pages such as glossaries are valuable and informative content, making them an excellent source of backlinks for your home service business. Resource pages are often designed to complement existing content from other websites and make it possible for you to demonstrate your expertise about the topic.

Brand Mentions

Brand mentions hold more significance than many website owners realize. While unlinked brand mentions may not provide immediate link juice to your website, they still contribute to your online reputation, visibility, and brand authority.

Unlinked brand mentions refer to instances where your brand is mentioned on another website or online platform but without a hyperlink that directs users to your website. These mentions may occur in various forms, such as a mention of your brand name, website, products, or services in the content or context of another website without any direct links.

Identifying these mentions and converting them into valuable backlinks will bolster your local authority and increase your visibility in the competitive online landscape.

Broken Link Opportunities

Another way to get links is to find broken links on other websites and reach out to them, asking if they would like to replace the broken links with links to your content instead. This requires some technical research, but with the help of an SEO tool, you can identify opportunities to get backlinks.

Other link building strategies include reaching out to influencers or industry experts for collaborations, participating in local events or organizations for local links, and leveraging the power of social media for link sharing.

Conclusion

Link building methods are comprehensive and require detailed planning and strategizing, followed by effective outreach and negotiation with potential partners in your local area.

Local links are essential to SEO because:

- They help you stand out from the crowd in your local community.
- Teaming up with other local businesses enhances your company's relevance and credibility.
- Online leads created from local link building will ultimately drive more traffic to your website and premises.
- You'll benefit from an increased conversion rate.
- They are critical for networking and forming business relationships with local businesses.

Keeping up with your local link building efforts will help sustain organic traffic to your website and keep your business visible to local clients.

CHAPTER 11: ADVANCED LOCAL SEO STRATEGIES

In this chapter, you'll get a better understanding of how all components work together and that SEO is a combination of signals. That includes:

- The importance of brand signals and online reviews
- Entity SEO and how AI is able to better understand who you are and what you do
- The increasing importance of video content in local search

In today's ever-evolving digital landscape, your home service business must adapt to the latest trends and techniques to maintain a competitive edge in local search engine optimization (SEO). While content creation and link building remain fundamental aspects of SEO, a deeper understanding of AI-driven search technologies necessitates the integration of brand signals, entities, and video into your local SEO strategy. This chapter will explore these crucial components and their impact on enhancing visibility, credibility, and customer engagement for home service businesses.

Brand Signals

Building trust and credibility brand signals are the digital footprints that signify the trust and credibility of your business. These include online reviews, social media presence, and consistent business information across various platforms. For home service businesses, building trust and credibility is paramount. Here's how to optimize your brand signals:

Online Reviews: Encourage satisfied customers to leave positive reviews on your Google Business Profile (GBP), Yelp, and other review platforms. Respond to reviews promptly to show that you value customer feedback. Example: An HVAC company could request reviews after completing a seasonal maintenance check, highlighting the importance of regular upkeep and customer satisfaction.

Social Media Presence: Maintain active profiles on major social media platforms. Share relevant content, such as completed projects, customer testimonials, and community involvement, to build a strong brand image. Example: A plumbing company can post before-and-after photos of a major pipe repair on Instagram, showcasing their expertise and the quality of their service.

Consistent Business Information: As outlined in prior chapters, ensure that your business name, address, and phone number (NAP) are consistent across all online directories and platforms. Inconsistent information can confuse search engines and customers, negatively impacting your local SEO. Example: An electrician must ensure that their NAP information is the same on their website, GBP, Yelp, Apple Maps and other directories to avoid discrepancies.

Enhancing Search Engine Relevance with Brand Signals

Search engines use brand signals to assess the relevance and authority of a business. A strong brand can significantly improve your ranking on search engine results pages (SERPs).

Implement these practices to enhance your search engine relevance:

Citations: Secure citations from reputable local directories and industry-specific websites. This reinforces your business's legitimacy and local relevance. Example: An appliance repair service can get listed in local business directories like Angie's List and HomeAdvisor to increase their local citations.

Quality Content: Develop high-quality content that addresses common customer queries and showcases your expertise. Blog posts, how-to guides, and case studies can establish your authority in the home services industry. Example: A handyman service could write a blog post on "10 Essential Tools Every Homeowner Should Have," providing useful information while subtly promoting their services.

Engage with Local Media: Appear in local news articles or sponsor community events. Media coverage can boost your brand's reputation and generate valuable backlinks. Example: An HVAC company could sponsor a local charity run and get featured in the local news, thereby improving its community presence and online authority.

Fostering local recognition and being recognized as a trusted local brand can lead to increased visibility and customer engagement. Here's how to strengthen your local presence:

Community Involvement: Participate in local events, charities, and sponsorships. Highlight these activities on your website and social media to demonstrate your commitment to the community. Example: An electrician could offer free electrical safety checks at a local community center and share photos and testimonials from the event on social media.

Local Listings: Ensure your business is listed on Google Business Profile, Bing Places, and Apple Maps. Optimize your listings with accurate information, high-quality images, and regular updates. Example: A plumbing company should regularly update its GBP profile with new photos of completed projects, special offers, and customer reviews.

Localized Content: Create content that is specifically tailored to your local audience. Highlight local projects, customer testimonials, and regional expertise to resonate with potential customers in your area. Example: An appliance repair service could write a case study highlighting how they helped a local restaurant keep their kitchen equipment in top shape, emphasizing their role in supporting local businesses.

Leveraging Entities for Improved Visibility Entity SEO

Leveraging entities focuses on optimizing for well-defined concepts or objects, helping search engines understand the context and meaning behind search queries. This semantic approach leads to more accurate and relevant search results. Implement these strategies to leverage entities:

Schema Markup: Implement structured data markup (schema) on your website to help search engines understand your content. Use relevant schemas such as LocalBusiness, Service, and Review to provide context and improve visibility in rich snippets and knowledge panels. Example: An HVAC company can use the Service schema to mark up details about their HVAC maintenance services, ensuring search engines accurately present this information in search results.

Entity-Based Content: Create content that clearly defines and addresses specific entities related to your services. This can include detailed service descriptions, FAQs, and glossaries that explain industry terms and concepts. Example: A plumber could create a comprehensive FAQ page addressing common questions about water heater installation and repair, providing clear, entity-specific information.

Optimize for Voice Search: With the rise of voice search, optimizing for entities becomes even more critical. Ensure your content is conversational and answers common voice search queries directly. Example: An electrician could optimize their content for voice search by including questions like, "How much does it cost to install a ceiling fan?" and providing a straightforward answer.

Enhancing visibility through entities by optimizing for entities, home service businesses can improve their visibility in search results. This increased visibility is crucial for capturing the attention of potential local customers. But how do you enhance your visibility?

Knowledge Graph: Aim to be featured in Google's Knowledge Graph by establishing your business as a recognized entity. This can be achieved through consistent branding, high-quality content, and authoritative backlinks. Example: A handyman service could aim to appear in the Knowledge Graph by creating detailed profiles on GBP, LinkedIn, and other platforms, coupled with quality backlinks from reputable sources.

Rich Snippets: Optimize your content for rich snippets by using structured data. Rich snippets can improve your click-through rates (CTR) by providing users with immediate answers to their queries directly in the SERPs. Example: An appliance repair service can use structured data to highlight customer ratings and service descriptions, increasing the chance of appearing in rich snippets for queries like "Best appliance repair near me."

Local Keywords: Incorporate local keywords that are relevant to your services and location. Use tools like Google Keyword Planner to identify popular search terms and phrases used by your local audience. Example: An HVAC company in Denver should target keywords such as "Dallas AC repair" or "Dallas heating services" in their web content and ads.

Adapting to evolving search technologies, the rise of AI-driven search features and voice search has made entity SEO increasingly important. These technologies rely on understanding entities and their relationships to provide accurate and contextually relevant answers. Look at how to adapt to these advancements:

Natural Language Processing (NLP): Optimize your content for NLP by writing in a clear, concise, and conversational manner. This helps search engines understand and interpret your content more effectively. Example: An HVAC company could write blog posts in a question-and-answer format, directly addressing typical customer inquiries in a natural, conversational style.

Voice Search Optimization: Focus on long-tail keywords and natural language queries that are commonly used in voice searches. Structure your content to provide direct answers to these queries. Example: A plumber could optimize for voice search by including content like "What to do if my pipes freeze" and providing a step-by-step guide.

AI Tools and Technologies: Leverage AI-powered tools such as chatbots and virtual assistants to enhance customer interaction and gather valuable data on customer preferences and behaviors. For example: An appliance repair service might use an AI chatbot on their website to answer common questions, book appointments, and guide customers through troubleshooting steps.

Leveraging video for engagement and SEO video content is highly engaging and can capture the attention of potential customers more effectively than text alone. Incorporate video into your local SEO strategy to increase your visibility and customer engagement.

Here's how video benefits your SEO efforts:

Showcase Your Work: Create videos that highlight completed projects, showcasing the quality and scope of your work. Before-and-after videos can be particularly impactful in demonstrating your expertise. For example: A remodeling company could create a video showcasing the transformation of a bathroom after a major renovation.

Explain Services: Produce informative videos that explain your services in detail. This can help potential customers better understand what you offer and how you can meet their needs. Example: An HVAC company could create a series of videos explaining the importance of regular HVAC maintenance and what customers can expect during a service visit.

Connect with the Audience: Use video to introduce your team, share customer testimonials, and provide behind-the-scenes glimpses of your business. This helps build a personal connection with your audience. Example: An electrician could film a day in the life of an electrician, showing the team at work and highlighting the safety measures they take.

Optimized video content for SEO videos can

improve SEO by increasing time spent on a website, reducing bounce rates, and providing additional opportunities for keyword optimization. Here's how to optimize your video content:

YouTube SEO: Create a YouTube channel and optimize each video with relevant titles, descriptions, tags, and thumbnails. Include local keywords to improve visibility in local search results. Example: An appliance repair service could create a YouTube video titled "How to Fix a Leaky Dishwasher in Nashville" to target local searchers.

Embed Videos on Your Website: Embed videos on relevant pages of your website to enhance user engagement and provide additional content for search engines to index. Example: A handyman service could embed tutorial videos on their service pages to help reduce bounce rates and keep visitors engaged.

Transcriptions and Captions: Provide transcripts and captions for your videos to make them accessible to a wider audience and improve keyword optimization. Example: An HVAC company could add captions to their instructional videos on YouTube, improving accessibility and keyword reach.

Localizing your video content by creating videos that highlight local projects, customer testimonials, or community involvement can strengthen a business's local presence. Here's how to focus your video content locally:

Local Projects: Feature local projects and success stories in your videos. Highlight the unique aspects of each project and how your services benefited the local community. Example: An electrician could create a video showing a major rewiring project at a local historical building, emphasizing their expertise in handling complex jobs.

Customer Testimonials: Record and share testimonials from satisfied local customers. Personal endorsements from recognizable local figures can significantly boost your credibility. Example: An HVAC company could film a satisfied customer discussing how their new air conditioning system improved their home's comfort during the hot summer months.

Community Involvement: Produce videos that showcase your participation in local events, charities, and sponsorships. This demonstrates your commitment to the community and fosters local goodwill. Example: A handyman service could create a video highlighting their participation in a local Habitat for Humanity build, showing their dedication to giving back to the community.

Conclusion

In summary, incorporating brand signals, entities,

and videos into your local SEO strategy is essential for home service businesses to thrive in 2024 and beyond. By building trust and credibility, optimizing for semantic understanding, and leveraging engaging video content, you can enhance your visibility, authority, and customer engagement in the local market. Strive to embrace these advanced strategies to stay ahead of the competition and drive more business to your doorstep.

CHAPTER 12: AI & GENERATIVE EXPERIENCE OPTIMIZATION

Welcome to the cutting edge of search for home service businesses, which started rolling out on May 14, 2024! In this chapter, we'll explore how artificial intelligence (AI) is reshaping search engines and what it means for your local business.

We're about to explore how you can harness these powerful technologies to boost your visibility and connect with more customers in your area.

The Rise of AI in Search

Remember when a Google search simply gave you a list of blue links? Those days are fading fast. Today, AI is revolutionizing how search engines understand and respond to user queries. Instead of just pointing to websites, search engines are now generating concise, informative summaries right on the results page.

What does this mean for you?

Well, imagine a potential customer in your city asking, "How do I fix a leaky faucet?" Instead of seeing a list of plumbing websites, they might get an AI-generated answer that explains the basics and potentially recommends local professionals (like you!) for more complex jobs.

What is Google's AI Overviews?

AI Overviews, which evolved from Search Generative Experience (SGE), is a technology that generates rich and concise summaries in response to user queries using advanced machine learning and natural language processing. This represents a shift from traditional search engine outcomes, which primarily provided lists of web pages.

According to a recent study by SEMrush, nearly 50% of Google searches now result in zero clicks, often due to users finding answers directly in AI-generated snippets. This trend highlights the growing importance of optimizing for AI-powered search results.

Key Features of AI-Powered Search:

1. **Contextualization**: AI understands the intent behind the query, not just the words.

2. **Synthesis**: It pulls information from multiple sources to create comprehensive answers.

3. **Engagement**: Responses are conversational, making the search experience more interactive with features to simplify, save, and further engage with the output.

How AI-Powered Search Works

Behind the scenes, AI-powered search operates through complex algorithms that analyze vast amounts of data. Here's a simplified breakdown:

1. **Data Collection**: AI gathers information from countless web pages, including your business listings and website.

2. **Preprocessing**: It cleans and organizes this data for analysis.

3. **Model Training**: Machine learning helps AI understand context, intent, and natural language.

4. **Response Generation**: AI will craft conversational summaries that directly address user queries.

5. **Continuous Improvement**: The system learns from user interactions and feedback to get better over time.

Impact on Home Service Businesses

This shift in search technology is a game-changer for local businesses like yours. Here's why:

1. **Increased Competition**: With AI-generated summaries, users might see information about multiple businesses at once. Standing out is more crucial than ever.

2. **Challenging Discovery**: If users get their answers directly in search results, they might not click through to websites as often. Your information needs to be prominently featured in these AI-generated responses.

3. **Trust Building**: Engaging, informative summaries can foster trust and relatability, potentially increasing your chances of winning new customers.

A study by BrightLocal found that 76% of consumers trust online reviews as much as personal recommendations. In the age of AI-powered search, these reviews can play a crucial role in how your business is presented in search results.

Optimizing for AI-Powered Search

So, how do you make sure your business shines in this new AI-powered landscape? Let's explore some strategies for what we'll call "Generative Experience Optimization" (GEO). While not an official term, GEO encompasses strategies to improve your visibility in AI-generated search results.

Key GEO Strategies for Home Service Businesses:

1. **Optimize for Specific Topics and Themes:** Use natural language phrases that reflect how people in your area actually search. For example, "emergency plumber in Detroit for burst pipes" rather than just "plumber Detroit."

2. **High-Quality, Structured Content:** Create detailed, valuable content that directly answers common customer questions. Use clear headings, bullet points, and short paragraphs to make your content easy for both humans and AI to understand.

3. **Implement Schema Markup:** This structured data helps search engines understand your content better, increasing your chances of appearing in rich snippets and AI-generated summaries.

4. **Encourage and Manage Reviews:** Customer reviews on your Google Business Profile and other platforms provide valuable

data for AI to use in generating summaries about your business.

5. **Diversify Your Content**: Use a mix of text, images, videos, and infographics. This caters to different user preferences and gives AI more ways to showcase your expertise.

6. **Mobile Optimization**: Ensure your website is mobile-friendly. According to Google, over 50% of global website traffic now comes from mobile devices.

7. **Monitor and Adapt**: Regularly analyze your performance in search results and be ready to adjust your strategy as AI technology evolves.

Best Practices

Let's get specific. Here are some best practices you can implement right away:

1. **Answer FAQs Directly**: Create a FAQ page that directly answers common questions about your services. Use conversational language that mirrors how people actually ask questions.

2. **Showcase Your Expertise**: Highlight your credentials, years of experience, and any awards or certifications. This helps establish

your authority to both AI and potential customers.

3. **Use Local References**: Mention local landmarks, events, or common issues specific to your area in your content. This signals strong local relevance to search engines.

4. **Create How-To Content**: Develop step-by-step guides for simple home maintenance tasks. This positions you as helpful and knowledgeable, even for jobs customers might do themselves.

5. **Utilize Video**: Create short, informative videos about common home service issues. Transcribe these videos and include the text on your site for AI to analyze.

6. **Build Quality Links**: Develop relationships with other local businesses or community organizations for mutually beneficial linking opportunities.

Measuring Your GEO Success

At the time of writing this book, Google AI Overviews data was not available in Google Search Console. Until any AI overview data becomes available in Google Search Console, you can monitor your positions, featured snippet opportunities, traffic, and click-through rates. Consider the following tactics.

Tactics that Work to Increase Visibility

- **Conversational Keywords**: Use natural language queries to align with how users phrase their questions.
- **Authority and Expertise**: Highlight credentials and customer testimonials to assert credibility.
- **Clear and Direct Answers**: Provide clear answers within the first few sentences to be captured by AI.
- **Use of Visual Aids**: Incorporate images and videos to enhance interaction and detail in your offerings.
- **Internal and External Linking**: Build a network of relevant internal and credible external links.
- **Cite Sources**: Add citations from credible sources.
- **Quotation Addition**: Include credible quotes.

- **Statistics Addition**: Provide quantitative statistics.
- **Fluency Optimization**: Improve the fluency of website text.
- **Easy-to-Understand**: Simplify the language of the website.

By employing these GEO strategies and tactics, local home service businesses can enhance visibility, engage potential customers more meaningfully, and remain competitive in an increasingly digital marketplace.

Challenges and Limitations of AI in Search

While AI-powered search offers many opportunities, it's important to be aware of its limitations:

1. **Potential for Bias**: AI systems can inadvertently perpetuate biases present in their training data. Stay vigilant and report any unfair representations you notice.
2. **Rapid Changes**: AI technology is evolving quickly. Strategies that work today might need adjustment tomorrow.
3. **Reduced Website Traffic**: As more queries are answered directly in search results, you

may see a decrease in website visits. Focus on optimizing for conversions when users do click through.

Ethical Considerations

As we embrace AI-powered search, it's crucial to consider its ethical implications. Ensure the information you provide online is accurate, unbiased, and representative of the diverse community you serve. Be transparent about your services and pricing, and never attempt to manipulate AI systems with false or misleading information.

Looking Ahead

The future of AI in search is exciting and full of potential. We may see more personalized results, increased use of voice search, and better integration with smart home devices. To stay ahead:

1. **Keep Learning**: Stay updated on AI and search engine developments.

2. **Experiment**: Don't be afraid to try new content formats or optimization techniques.

3. **Focus on Value**: Above all, prioritize providing genuine value to your customers.

Conclusion

The integration of AI into search engines represents a fundamental shift in how potential customers find and interact with local home service businesses like yours. By understanding and optimizing for AI-powered search, you can stay ahead of the curve and ensure your business remains visible and competitive in this new digital landscape.

Remember, the key is to provide valuable, relevant, and easily accessible information that addresses your customers' needs. Do this consistently, and you'll be well-positioned to thrive in the age of AI-powered search.

CHAPTER 13: VOICE SEARCH OPTIMIZATION FOR YOUR LOCAL BUSINESS

Voice search has emerged as a pivotal tool for your local business, fundamentally altering how you engage with customers and optimize your digital presence.

- Voice search usage in-home services has grown by approximately 25% year-over-year since 2020.

- Businesses optimized for voice search have seen a 20% increase in website traffic compared to non-optimized competitors.

- Voice search leads have a 30% higher conversion rate than traditional search leads for local businesses.

- 55% of millennials use voice search daily, making it a crucial channel for reaching younger homeowners.

The key to success in voice search optimization is to think like your customer and provide clear, concise, and helpful information that directly addresses their needs.

With a significant portion of voice searches carrying local intent, it's imperative for you to adapt your SEO strategies to capture this growing segment of potential customers. Let's dive into the key changes, impacts, and strategies you must adopt to thrive in the era of voice search.

Changes and Impacts of Voice Search for Your Business

Local Intent and Discoverability

Imagine a homeowner with a burst pipe frantically asking their smart speaker, "Find an emergency plumber near me!" Your business needs to be ready to answer that call. Recent studies suggest that approximately 40-50% of voice searches are aimed at finding local information, such as "electrician near me" or "best handyman in Dallas." This trend underscores the necessity for you to optimize your digital presence to be easily discoverable via voice search.

Conversational and Long Queries

Voice searches differ significantly from traditional

text-based searches; they're typically longer and more conversational. For example, while a text search might be "best HVAC service," a voice search could be "Who provides the best HVAC service near me?" This shift requires you to rethink your traditional keyword-focused SEO strategies to incorporate natural language processing and user intent.

Enhanced Local SEO Importance

Given that many voice searches are location-specific, your local SEO has become more vital than ever. If you have a complete and accurate Google Business Profile listing, you're more likely to appear in voice search results for location-based inquiries. This involves ensuring accurate and comprehensive local listings and tailoring your content to local search terms and questions.

Impact on Consumer Behavior

Voice search optimization can magnify the influence of your positive customer reviews and ratings. If your business has excellent reviews, you can expect higher consumer trust and increased spending. This highlights the importance of reputation management, as voice assistants often pull from review sites and Google listings to provide recommendations.

New Strategies for Your Local Business

1. Optimize for Conversational Keywords

To effectively leverage voice search, you need to identify and integrate conversational keywords and phrases into your content. Think about how people naturally speak and frame their questions. Tools like AnswerThePublic and Google's People Also Ask can aid in understanding these natural language queries.

PRO TIP: Implement local SEO best practices on your website to naturally optimize your business for "near me" phrases.

2. Create FAQ Pages

FAQ pages are ideal for voice search optimization as they provide direct answers to common questions in a straightforward manner. Structure your website to include an extensive, well-thought-out FAQ section to improve your chances of appearing in voice search results.

PRO TIP: Optimize your Google Business Profile FAQs to directly address common voice queries.

3. Leverage Schema Markup

Implementing schema markup helps search engines understand the context of your content, thereby enhancing its chances of appearing in rich snippets. This structured data can improve your visibility in voice search results, making it easier for voice assistants to extract and present your information to users.

4. Focus on Micro-Moments

Micro-moments occur when consumers want immediate information or action, such as "I need a locksmith now" or "Where can I buy paint nearby?" By understanding and optimizing for these instances, you can better meet consumer needs and drive conversions. Create time-sensitive and location-specific content that answers immediate user queries.

5. Enhance Mobile Friendliness and Site Speed

Voice searches are frequently conducted on mobile devices, making mobile optimization crucial. Ensure that your website is mobile-friendly and loads quickly for a positive user experience and better search rankings. Use Google's Mobile-Friendly Test and PageSpeed Insights to assess and improve your site's mobile performance.

Future Direction for Voice Search Optimization

Personalization and Context Awareness

Voice assistants are becoming increasingly personalized, delivering search results based on user preferences, behaviors, and past interactions. This trend will likely continue, necessitating you to tailor your offerings and interactions to individual user needs. Leverage customer data to offer personalized recommendations and significantly enhance user engagement and satisfaction.

Integration with IoT

The integration of voice search with Internet of Things (IoT) devices is deepening, enabling users to control smart home devices, connected cars, and more through voice commands. Consider how your services can integrate with IoT devices to offer seamless, voice-activated solutions.

Expansion in Emerging Markets

Voice search adoption is accelerating in emerging markets, driven by smartphone growth and advancements in speech recognition technology. To tap into these new audiences, you may need to optimize for various languages and cultural preferences. This could involve creating multilingual content and understanding regional search behaviors.

Conclusion

Voice search is rapidly becoming an essential component of your local business strategy. By focusing on local SEO, conversational content, and customer engagement, you can remain competitive in the evolving digital landscape. As voice search technology continues to advance, staying informed about the latest trends and best practices will be crucial for maintaining a strong online presence and capturing the growing number of voice search users.

Implementing these strategies will not only enhance your visibility in voice search results but also improve overall customer satisfaction and drive more conversions, ensuring your business thrives in the voice-first world of 2024 and beyond.

CHAPTER 14: THE FUTURE OF LOCAL SEO FOR HOME SERVICES

Congratulations! You've reached the final chapter of our book on local SEO for home service business owners. We've covered a lot, from on-page and off-page SEO to technical and local strategies. Now, let's pivot to some of the advanced trends and emerging technologies shaping the future of SEO.

The Influence of Generative AI and Voice Search

The advent of generative AI has introduced groundbreaking concepts transforming local SEO. These AI-driven advancements go beyond traditional search functions, aiming to create meaningful and productive user experiences. Voice search, driven by AI, has significantly impacted how users interact with search engines, making natural language and conversational search more prevalent.

Voice Search and Conversational Search

With the growing popularity of voice-activated devices like Amazon Alexa and Google Home, optimizing for voice search is crucial. Users tend to use longer, more conversational queries when using voice search, as opposed to the more concise keywords used in text searches. This means businesses need to adapt their content to cater to these natural language queries.

Here's how SGE can change a simple search query like "sewer repair near me" into a more complex, conversation-like interaction:

Initial Query: "drain company that specializes in sewer repair in Edmonton"

Follow-up Query: "list the companies that are experienced working with clay tile sewers"

Further Refinement: "rank the companies by how long they have been in business or the number of reviews they have"

This kind of interaction shows that businesses need to keep their descriptions, images, and reviews up-to-date, as these elements will directly influence how they appear in search results. Use real perspectives, data, and unique insights to engage users and meet their search needs.

PRO TIP: Businesses need to become more location- and service-specific and have more assets (images and videos) to help AI understand and accurately represent their offerings.

Becoming a Subject-Matter Expert: Entity SEO

Search engines are increasingly focused on understanding entities—distinct and well-defined objects or concepts like locations, people, or businesses. Positioning yourself and your business as a subject-matter expert will become more crucial. This involves creating comprehensive and authoritative content that showcases your business's expertise, helping you improve visibility in SERPs and attract targeted organic traffic. Entities will continue to be adaptive to new search methods and will help search engines better understand the context and meaning behind search queries, moving beyond keywords.

New Google Business Profile Features

Google Business Profiles continue to evolve, providing more ways for local businesses to connect with customers. Increased integrations with existing service providers for chat, messaging, and scheduling are becoming more prevalent. The continued importance of Google reviews and other platforms in Unified Reviews will be displayed, making reputation management crucial. Being responsive to customer inquiries on these platforms will, as always, continue to be important.

Content Repurposing: Maximizing Your Assets

Repurposing content allows you to extend the life and reach of your existing assets. Adapt your blog posts into different formats like videos, checklists, and photos to cater to various audience preferences. This strategy not only maximizes your content's value but also amplifies your brand message across multiple platforms, including social media, thereby attracting a wider audience.

Emerging Technologies in Local Search

Voice Search Optimization

With voice-activated devices like Amazon Alexa and Google Home gaining in popularity, optimizing for voice search is crucial. This means using natural language and a conversational tone in your content to match how people speak their queries.

Google Lens and Image Search

Google Lens is a powerful tool that allows users to search for products and services using images. For instance, a user can take a picture of a piece of furniture and immediately see similar products and where to buy them. For home service businesses, this technology can be leveraged to showcase completed projects. For example, a picture of custom-built-ins can help users find local carpenters who can create similar pieces.

Augmented Reality (AR)

AR provides immersive experiences by overlaying digital information in the real world. Home service businesses can use AR to create virtual experiences that showcase their services, thereby enhancing user engagement and visibility in local search results.

Geo-Targeting and Geofencing

Geo-targeting and geofencing allow businesses to deliver targeted messages based on a user's real-time location. This can drive foot traffic and conversions by reaching customers as they enter a defined area around your business.

Video in Local Search

Video content is becoming increasingly important in local search strategies. Consumers prefer video over traditional text-based content, which means businesses need to create engaging videos that highlight their brand and services. Optimizing video content for search engines is crucial, including using relevant keywords and ensuring videos are mobile-friendly. Better mobile devices and AI editing tools make creating and posting video content easier to businesses to create videos. Posting videos on platforms like Google My Business and local directories, and promoting them through social media and paid ads, can enhance local visibility and engagement.

Existing Players Integrating Local Search and New Market Entrants

The landscape of local search is becoming more diverse, with both existing players integrating advanced features and new players entering the market. Companies like Meta AI and custom AI models are pushing the boundaries of what local search can achieve. New search engines like Perplexity AI are emerging, offering innovative search experiences. Additionally, Apple Maps and Bing are advancing their local business profile features, further enriching user interactions.

The Impact on Home Service Businesses

Increased Visibility and Engagement

Leveraging emerging technologies can enhance your business's visibility in local search results and improve customer engagement, leading to higher conversion rates and better customer retention.

Improved Customer Experience

Technologies like AR and voice search offer more interactive and convenient ways for customers to access information and services, thereby enhancing their overall experience.

Competitive Advantage

Early adoption of new technologies can differentiate your business in the market, providing you with a competitive edge and meeting the evolving expectations of tech-savvy consumers.

Future Expectations

AI and Machine Learning Integration

As AI technologies advance, we can expect more personalized and predictive local search experiences, catering to individual user preferences and behaviors.

Expansion of AR Applications

The use of augmented reality in local search is likely to expand, providing more immersive ways for consumers to explore products and services.

Continued Growth of Voice Search

Voice search optimization will remain essential, necessitating ongoing efforts to ensure your business remains visible in voice search results.

Continued Integration of SEO

Search engine optimization will become even more crucial, with businesses increasingly integrating SEO into their ongoing operations. Staying updated with best practices and consistently applying them will be key to maintaining visibility and competitiveness.

Conclusion

SEO is a dynamic field that demands continuous learning and adaptation. Embrace new features like generative AI with Search Generative Experience (SGE), entity SEO, content repurposing, and the latest advancements in local search technologies. Stay curious, keep up with trends, and never stop experimenting. By doing so, you can position your home service business as a local market leader and drive consistent success.

Thank you for joining us on this journey through the world of local SEO. We hope this book has provided you with the knowledge and tools necessary to achieve measurable success in the digital realm.

Good luck with your SEO endeavors, and may your online presence shine brightly in the competitive local market!

RESOURCES & ADDITIONAL SOURCES

Google. “Search Quality Evaluator Guidelines”

https://static.googleusercontent.com/media/guidelines.raterhub.com/en//searchqualityevaluatorguidelines.pdf

Google. “A New Way to Search With Generative AI” https://static.googleusercontent.com/media/www.google.com/en//search/howsearchworks/google-about-SGE.pdf

Google. “Guidelines for representing your business on Google”

https://support.google.com/business/answer/3038177?hl=en

Google. “All Business Profile policies & guidelines”

https://support.google.com/business/answer/7667250?hl=en

Creating helpful, reliable, people-first content

https://developers.google.com/search/docs/fundamentals/creating-helpful-content#get-to-know-e-a-t-and-the-quality-rater-guidelines

Search Engine Optimization (SEO) Starter Guide

https://developers.google.com/search/docs/fundamentals/seo-starter-guide

Local Consumer Review Survey 2023

https://www.brightlocal.com/research/local-consumer-review-survey/

ABOUT THE AUTHOR

Matt Miciula is a passionate digital marketer and local SEO specialist dedicated to empowering home service businesses. With over a decade of experience in the industry, Matt possesses a unique combination of technical expertise and creative flair.

His passion for helping small businesses thrive in a digital landscape led him to conduct extensive research and develop practical strategies tailored to the unique needs of the home services sector, which he calls the Digital Shift Method. Matt and his team have helped numerous home service businesses implement this proven formula to optimize their online visibility and gain a competitive edge.

Matt's approach to SEO is rooted in his dedication to staying up-to-date with the latest industry trends and best practices. His love for technology, understanding algorithms and unraveling the secrets of search engines led him to establish Digital Shift as a go-to resource in the field of local SEO for home services.

When he is not immersed in the world of SEO, Matt enjoys exploring the great outdoors, spending time with his family, and practicing photography. He resides in Calgary, Alberta, Canada, with his beloved children and wife.